westermann

On Track
Workbook

Englisch für Gymnasien

6

von:
Annie Altamirano
Annie Cornford
Jon Hird
Helga Holtkamp

herausgegeben von:
Helga Holtkamp

Lehrwerk und weitere Begleitmaterialien:

Schulbuch ISBN 978-3-14-040326-9
Medienpaket ISBN 978-3-14-062684-2
Klassenarbeitstrainer ISBN 978-3-7426-0336-4

 **BiBox – Digitale Unterrichtsmaterialien**
Nähere Informationen unter www.bibox.schule

Vokabel-Apps sind online erhältlich.

© 2024 Westermann Bildungsmedien Verlag GmbH, Georg-Westermann-Allee 66, 38104 Braunschweig
www.westermann.de

Das Werk und seine Teile sind urheberrechtlich geschützt. Jede Nutzung in anderen als den gesetzlich zugelassenen bzw. vertraglich zugestandenen Fällen bedarf der vorherigen schriftlichen Einwilligung des Verlages. Nähere Informationen zur vertraglich gestatteten Anzahl von Kopien finden Sie auf www.schulbuchkopie.de.

Für Verweise (Links) auf Internet-Adressen gilt folgender Haftungshinweis: Trotz sorgfältiger inhaltlicher Kontrolle wird die Haftung für die Inhalte der externen Seiten ausgeschlossen. Für den Inhalt dieser externen Seiten sind ausschließlich deren Betreiber verantwortlich. Sollten Sie daher auf kostenpflichtige, illegale oder anstößige Inhalte treffen, so bedauern wir dies ausdrücklich und bitten Sie, uns umgehend per E-Mail davon in Kenntnis zu setzen, damit beim Nachdruck der Verweis gelöscht wird.

Druck A[1] / Jahr 2024
Alle Drucke der Serie A sind inhaltlich unverändert.

Unter Mitarbeit von: Christine House, Sîan Jones

Umschlaggestaltung: Detlef Möller, Paderborn
Cover vorne: © Serge Bertasius Photography / Shutterstock.com. Edinburgh city centre at night
Cover hinten: © Molchanov, Dmitry / Shutterstock.com
Druck und Bindung: Westermann Druck GmbH, Georg-Westermann-Allee 66, 38104 Braunschweig

ISBN 978-3-14-**040346**-7

How to work with the Workbook

On Track 6 Workbook has three regular workshops. Every page in your workbook belongs to a page in your students' book. There is a reference at the top of the page (→ **students' book, page 12**, etc.). The colours of the pages are also the same. The activities and exercises have numbers, letters and symbols as in your students' book. You will also find webcodes.

How to use the webcodes

A webcode is like a small website. All the *On Track* audio material that you need for class or homework is here: www.westermann.de/webcode. You can also find transcripts of the audios and videos. You can listen online or download a folder with everything in it. Type in the code for the workshop (**WES-40346-001**) without the @ and click on the lock button to get to the page for Workshop 1. You know the webcodes from your students' book.

These are the webcodes in *On Track 6 Workbook*:
Workshop 1: @ WES-40346-001   Workshop 2: @ WES-40346-002   Workshop 3: @ WES-40346-003

> The **grammar appendix** explains all the grammar that you revise and learn in *On Track 6*. The grammar appendix in your workbook and students' book are identical. You can, for example, collect the grammar pages from the workbook in a folder to look up certain grammar points and aspects.

There are also eight grammar videos on the most important grammar topics in English.
You can find them under the webcode for your students' book

- The passive (Video 3, WES-40326-001)
- Reported speech (Video 4, WES-40326-001)
- Gerund and infinitives (Video 7, WES-40326-001)
- *If*-sentences 1 and 2 (Video 10, WES-40326-001)
- *If*-sentences 3 (Video 14, WES-40326-002)
- The present perfect (Video 16, WES-40326-002)
- Past tenses (Video 21, WES-40326-003)
- Future tenses (Video 24, WES-40326-003)

Contents

Workshop 1: India — page 6

PART 1

Page	Topic	Grammar	Activities
6	India and the British	The passive (G 2)	Watch a video. Complete a text with the correct forms.
8	Practice: A book about India / Writing focus		Complete a text with the correct forms. Read a text. Listen to a text. Write a short text.
11	Passive resistance	Reported speech (G 3)	Read an interview and write a summary. Complete a text. Write definitions for words. Watch a video.
13	Practice: You're not alone / Viewing focus		Read a report. Explain words. Watch a video. Report what someone said.
16	Recognizing text types		Prepare a leaflet for a campaign.

PART 2

Page	Topic	Grammar	Activities
17	Slum life	Gerunds and infinitives (G 4)	Complete a text with the correct forms. Listen to a podcast. Read a summary and answer questions.
19	Practice: Films about India / Reading focus		Listen to study notes. Listen to a conversation. Complete a text with the correct forms.
22	Traditional and modern cultures	If-sentences type 1 and 2 (G 5)	Complete a text with the correct forms. Summarize the main points of a text.
24	Practice: Sounds of India / Speaking focus		Listen to a conversation. Complete a text. Do research. Watch a music video. Read a conversation and answer questions.
27	Preparing to write a text		Write an article.

PART 3

Page	Topic
28	Mediation
30	My review

Workshop 2: South Africa — page 31

PART 1

Page	Topic	Grammar	Activities
31	Hi from Jozi!	Relative clauses (G 6)	Complete a text. Listen to a radio programme. Do a quiz.
33	Practice: Accept and respect / Viewing focus		Read a text. Complete a text with the correct forms. Watch a video. Write a review.
36	Sports and politics	Modals (G 7) If-sentences type 3 (G 5)	Listen to a conversation. Read an article. Choose headings. Complete sentences with the correct forms.
38	Practice: Headline news / Reading focus		Complete a text with the correct forms. Listen to a podcast. Read an article and answer questions.
40	Analysing an extract		Analyse an extract.

PART 2

Page	Topic	Grammar	Activities
41	Wildlife in South Africa	Present perfect and present perfect progressive (G 1)	Complete a text. Choose a heading. Explain the meaning of words. Listen to an interview and complete sentences.

PART 2	44	Practice: Making a difference / Writing focus		Listen to a radio interview. Complete a text with the correct forms. Write a magazine advert.
	46	Music matters	Modals (G 7)	Read a conversation and answer questions. Listen to a podcast. Write a text.
	48	Practice: South African style / Speaking focus		Complete a text. Watch a video. Read an article. Explain the meaning of words and phrases. Write a description. Listen to two students.
	51	Analysing song lyrics		Watch a video. Read lyrics and find literary devices.
PART 3	52	Mediation		
	54	My review		

	55	**Workshop 3: Into the future**		
PART 1	55	Living together	Past tenses (G 1)	Read a report and answer questions. Complete a text. Listen to a podcast.
	58	Practice: Being yourself / Speaking focus		Complete a text. Listen to a conversation/a presentation/a song. Write a text/an article. Talk to a partner. Watch a video.
	61	Rethinking climate change	Future tenses (G 1) Conjunctions with time clauses (G 8)	Brainstorm a topic. Complete a text. Watch a video. Explain a graphic.
	63	Practice: Getting our future back / Viewing focus		Complete a text. Watch a video.
	66	Assessing claims		Read short texts. Assess claims. Write a report.
PART 2	67	Back to the future	Future tenses (G 1) Question tags (G 9)	Watch a video. Do research. Read a book review. Complete a text/sentences. Write a short text.
	70	Practice: Speaking out / Writing focus		Listen to a tourist guide's talk/to a conversation. Complete a text/sentences. Find words. Put text paragraphs in the right order. Write an article.
	73	World English	Quantifiers (G 10)	Complete a text/sentences. Explain the meaning of words. Watch a video.
	75	Practice: Broadening your horizons / Reading focus		Listen to a conversation. Explain the meaning of words and phrases. Answer questions. Read and complete a text.
	79	Reporting on fake news		Listen to a conversation. Read an article. Summarize your assessment.
PART 3	80	Mediation		
	82	My review		
	83	Grammar		
	106	Acknowledgements		

five 5

India and the British

1 The British Empire

a Watch how India became the biggest and most significant of all Britain's colonies. Decide whether the statements are true or false and correct the false ones.

		True	False
1	Clive believed fighting was more rewarding than being an office worker.	☐	☐
2	The ruler of Bengal was defeated in the Battle of Plassey.	☐	☐
3	'Loot' referred to the riches that were stolen from the East India Company.	☐	☐
4	New palaces in Calcutta were built to look like grand buildings in Britain.	☐	☐
5	Clive's hunger for power and wealth built other empires around the world.	☐	☐

_____

_____

b Match the words with the definitions.

1 dominate	A great wealth	1 _____
2 ambitious	B place to keep riches	2 _____
3 outsmart	C win by using tricks	3 _____
4 challenge	D have control	4 _____
5 treasury	E eager to succeed	5 _____
6 fortune	F oppose or compete	6 _____

2 The superlatives of India. Complete the text with the superlative form of the adjectives from the box. There is one adjective you do not need.

> amazing ■ dangerous ■ high ■ holy ■ large ■ long ■ ugly ■ wild

Did you know that, at 2,704 km, the Ganges is _____ (1) river in India? It rises in the Himalayas, the mountain range with many of the earth's _____ peaks. India's _____ (3) river, which is sacred to Hindu people, flows into the Bay of Bengal in a region called the Sundarbans, which is among _____ (4) river deltas in the world. Apparently, it is _____ (5) place to visit, but one of _____ (6) and _____ (7), too, because it is the home of the man-eating Royal Bengal Tiger.

Workshop 1

→ students' book, pages 14/15

3 **The Partition of British India.** Complete the text with the correct passive form of the verbs in brackets.

When independence _____ (1) (*grant*) to the former imperial domain of British India in 1947, it _____ (2) (*partition*) into two countries: India and Pakistan.

Attempts to grant self-rule to the Indians _____ (3) (*debate*) since the early 1900s and resulted in the Indian Councils Act of 1909 and the Government of India Act of 1919. In 1935, the Government of India Act constituted a number of provinces with their own legislatures where representatives _____ (4) (*elect*).

In 1945, the Labour Party came to power in Britain and solemnly promised to grant independence to India. Their plan _____ (5) (*develop*) on the basis of the 1935 Act. Elections _____ (6) (*hold*) in all the provinces of British India, and the Muslim League won all the seats reserved for Muslims. In 1946, a Cabinet Mission _____ (7) (*send*) to India by the British Government.

A confederation and provinces in three regions _____ (8) (*propose*). The Muslim community pushed for a separate nation as the only way to safeguard their identity. Riots spread through Calcutta and Bombay and, on 9 December 1946, the Muslim League withdrew its support for the Cabinet Mission, claiming that the rights of the Muslim minority _____ (9) (*not respect*) in the Assembly.

A separate nation for Muslims _____ (10) (*demand*) by various Muslim leaders in the previous decades. The Partition Scheme _____ (11) (*outline*) in April 1947 and, on 4 June, the scheme _____ (12) (*announce*) on the All India Radio.

The drawing of the boundary was extremely difficult, and thousands of families _____ (13) (*force*) to leave the land they had inhabited for generations. Law and order broke down and there was large scale violence. In the Punjab and Bengal region, refugees moved from one side to the other, in search of safety.

The Partition of India was one of the most defining events in the history of the Indian subcontinent. It _____ (14) (*estimate*) that up to 20 million people _____ (15) (*affect*) by the Partition and between 200,000 and 1 million lost their lives.

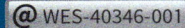

The seven Indian leaders accept the plan for the transition of power

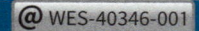

Practice: A book about India

4 Origins of Indian literature. Complete the summary about the origins of Indian literature.

> amount ■ anthem ■ dialects ■ government ■ languages ■ literature ■
> period ■ poetry ■ richness ■ writer

Indian _____ (1) dates back to 1500 – 1200 BCE and is one of the oldest in the world. It is composed of 22 officially recognized _____ (2) and it is characterized by its poetic _____ (3). In the medieval _____ (4), Persian and Urdu were used by the educated and the _____ (5), while Bengali and various _____ (6) of Hindi, Persian and Urdu began to appear. Nobel laureate Rabindranath Tagore is the most well-known Bengali _____ (7). He composed the national _____ (8) of India and Bangladesh. Bengali is the second most commonly spoken language in India and has produced an incredible _____ (9) of literature, _____ (10) and songs.

5 Indian literature during British rule. Now read this text and do the tasks.

> Indian English literature emerged during British rule when English was introduced to India. Its roots can be traced back to the late 19th and early 20th centuries when English education was established in cities like Madras, Bombay and Calcutta.
> Raja Ram Mohan Roy, a Bengal social reformer, pioneered Indian writing in English, producing political pamphlets supporting Indian independence. He believed English should be India's medium of education to be recognized on the global stage. In the early 20th century, a group of British writers who were born or brought up in India, including Rudyard Kipling, Jim Corbett, and George Orwell, wrote with Indian themes but in a primarily occidental style, creating renowned works like 'Kim' and 'The Jungle Book'.
> Indian English literature initially drew inspiration from colonial and Western philosophies, leading to popular novels and stories exploring new themes. Writers like Tagore demonstrated the Indian writers' ability to express themselves effortlessly in a foreign language. This literature also catalysed social change, challenging orthodox norms and advocating for women's education and an end to practices like sati. During the freedom struggle, Indian English literature expressed native sentiments against the British Empire, with leaders like Mahatma Gandhi and Jawaharlal Nehru wielding the English language to elevate its prominence in British India to one of excellence and merit.

1 Explain the role played by the cities of Madras, Bombay and Calcutta.
2 Outline the importance of Raja Ram Mohan Roy.

Workshop 1

→ students' book, pages 16/17

3 Describe the characteristics of the writers of the early 20th century. Give examples.
4 Explain western education's impact on native writers and Indian society.
5 Explain how politics influenced Indian literature and the use of English.
6 Research and explain what *sati* is.

6 Kamala Das, 'the mother of modern Indian poetry'

a Complete the text with the verbs in brackets in the correct tense. Use active or passive forms, modals and the passive with *get* when necessary.

Indian women poets writing in English _____ (1) (*reveal*) the mind-boggling variety of themes and style that poetry can offer. Over the last fifty years, [...] these poets have tried to speak in a distinctly personal voice, yet they are a collective voice asserting the autonomy of women.

[...] Kamala Das [...] was one of the most prominent feminist voices of the postcolonial era and _____ (2) (*consider*) to be the mother of modern Indian English poetry. She _____ (3) (*write*) in her mother tongue Malayalam and English. Kamala Das was born in 1934. Her childhood _____ (4) (*spend*) in the family home in Malabar, Kerala and Calcutta where her father worked. Kamala Das _____ (5) (*belong*) to a family who _____ (6) (*consider*) literary royalty in Kerala. Her mother was a famous poet and her great uncle a respected writer. [...] Married at the age of 15, she had to find a way to pursue her passion for writing while being weighed down by the expectations of her 'duties' as a wife and mother. [...] With her poems, she tried to give voice to a generation of women who _____ (7) (*confine*) to their households and _____ (8) (*view*) as a commodity. In her poems, she _____ (9) (*portray*) [...] women [...] as human, with desires, pain and emotions just like men. [...] She _____ herself _____ (10) (*hire*) as a columnist in a popular weekly and managed _____ her articles _____ (11) (*publish*) despite her father's formidable opposition.

In 1988, 15 years after her autobiography *Ente Kadha* _____ (12) (*first appear*) in Malayalam, it _____ (13) (*translate*) into English with the title *My Story*. [...]

Kamala Das _____ (14) (*shortlist*) for the Nobel Prize for Literature in 1984. Much of her work _____ (15) (*publish*) in foreign languages including French and German. She died in Pune, on 31st May 2009, at the age of 75.

Source (abbreviated and adapted): Sheryl Sebastian, "Kamala Das – The Mother of Modern Indian English Poetry", Feminism in India, 31 March 2017, https://feminisminindia.com/2017/03/31/kamala-das-essay/ [29.08.2023]

b Find the words for these definitions. The order is the same as in the text.

1 extremely surprising and difficult to understand or imagine _____

2 in a clearly noticeable way _____

3 burdened with problems and difficulties _____

4 anything that can be bought and sold _____

7 WRITING FOCUS: Getting to know India

a Listen to the information and number the photos (1 – 4) in the order you hear about them.

A ☐

B ☐

C ☐

D ☐

b Choose one of the photos that interests you. Listen again and note down as many facts as you can remember about it. Then do some more research and write a short text about it (150 words).

8 Indian films. Have you seen a film by an Indian filmmaker? If you have, give the title and write a short description of what film is about. If you have not, do some research and choose a title. Look for information about it and write a short text (150 words).

Passive resistance

9 **Ghandi's legacy.** Read Sam's (S) interview with Ash (A) and Frances (F). Then write a summary of the interview. Use reported speech and at least four of these reporting verbs:
agree, ask, believe, note, point out, say, want to know.

S   Welcome back to *Four Corners*! Today, we have Ash and Frances with us to share their thoughts on Gandhi. So, Gandhi's non-violent approach to political change played a significant role in India's struggle for independence. What are your thoughts on his philosophy of non-violence?

A   I truly admire his philosophy of non-violence. It shows peaceful resistance can achieve profound results, and it paved the way for social justice movements around the world.

F   I agree with Ash. Gandhi's commitment to non-violence is inspiring.

S   Absolutely, his principles have indeed had a global impact. Ash, how do you think Gandhi's leadership and doctrine of 'satyagraha' influenced other movements worldwide?

A   Gandhi's leadership and 'satyagraha' had a profound influence on many movements promoting civil rights and fighting against oppression. His legacy has transcended borders and continues to guide those seeking equality.

S   Well said, Ash. Frances, Gandhi's early life experiences in Natal, South Africa, played a pivotal role in shaping his activism. What are your thoughts on this period of his life?

F   Gandhi's experiences in Natal were transformative. They exposed him to racial discrimination and injustice, which fuelled his determination to fight for a more just society. It's impressive how these events shaped his path as a leader.

S   Indeed, his journey had a significant impact on his future endeavours. Lastly, I'd like to ask you how you believe Gandhi's legacy continues to resonate in the world today.

A   Gandhi's legacy remains alive through various social justice movements that emphasize non-violence as a means to create positive change. His teachings inspire people to stand up for justice and equality.

F   I agree. Gandhi's legacy serves as a reminder that peaceful and compassionate actions can lead to significant transformations in society. His principles are timeless and relevant even today.

S   Thank you both for sharing your insightful thoughts on Gandhi and his lasting impact. It's clear that his philosophy of non-violence and commitment to justice continue to inspire young people in their attempts to make the world a better place.

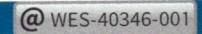

10 Controversial statues

a Read about the controversy surrounding monuments and statues and complete the text with the letters A – D for the phrases below.

A temples get sacked
B represented through those monuments
C of what the rest of us should be doing
D including memorials and monuments

Statues and monuments that have long honoured the memory of personalities of the past have stood for more than a century. However, some people may ask themselves: Why do we have monuments and **memorials**? What purpose do they serve in society?
According to some historians, monuments of people come out of a tradition of imitation.
The idea is that a statue of a civil leader could represent someone whose virtue or deeds we should **emulate** as citizens. They are held up as a model of **civic identity**, _____ (1). What we choose to memorialize speaks to our values as a society, and often, certain populations are excluded entirely from that. Following the murder of George Floyd, protests against racism and police violence have renewed attention on the **legacies** of injustices, _____ (2). People have been asking: Does this statue still need to be here? Debate around the removal of memorials and monuments that honour people whose causes are considered offensive to **marginalized** groups has been a **hot-button issue** of late. A historian who specializes in the rhetoric of public art, _____ (3), said such controversy is as old as time. '**Iconoclasm** is not new; it's been going on for thousands of years in different circumstances,' she said. 'Basically, any time a new government or **regime** or religion comes in, stuff gets torn down, _____ (4). What that signals is a shift in power.'

b Write explanations or definitions for the words in **bold** in your own words.

11 No place in our city

a In 2020, the bronze statue of Edward Colston was pulled from its plinth and pushed into Bristol docks by protesters. Watch the video and put the arguments for and against this action into two columns.

Honouring slave traders is wrong and action is justifiable.	
FOR	AGAINST

b Think of a statue (or a place or a street name) you know in Germany and say why you think it should / shouldn't stay. You can also do some research about re-naming controversies in the media. Write about 150 words together.

Practice: You're not alone

12 **Islamophobia in the UK**

a Read this report about Islamophobia and outline the main points it makes.

The publication of statistics by the British Home Office in 2022 showed Islamophobic hate crimes in England and Wales skyrocketed last year. Muslims were the most targeted group with 3,459 crimes, a 42% increase
5 since 2021.
A London-based charity that helps Muslims facing Islamophobia says people are being bullied and harassed at work because of their religion. Some people they interviewed with first-hand experience of
10 this had some pretty horrific stories to tell.
Young Muslims living in the UK also face an enormous social mobility challenge and are being held back from reaching their full potential at every stage in life, a report by an independent advisory body has found. The report uncovers significant barriers to improved social
15 mobility for young Muslims from school through university and into the workplace.
The report found that young people from Pakistani and Bangladeshi backgrounds are more likely to succeed in education and go on to university than other groups – particularly girls. However, this did not translate into the labour market, and Muslims experience the greatest economic disadvantages of any faith group in UK society.
20 A team of academics explored young Muslims' perceptions and experiences of growing up and seeking work in Britain. Participants expressed a strong sense of work ethic, high resilience and a desire to succeed in school and beyond. But many felt they must work 'ten times as hard' as non-Muslims just to get the same opportunities due to cultural differences and various forms of discrimination.
25 They also reported that teachers often had stereotypical expectations of them. They argued that there are insufficient numbers of Muslim teachers or role models in schools and they are given inadequate individual tailored support, guidance and encouragement.
In higher education, young Muslims are more likely to drop out early or to gain fewer 'good degrees'. Interviewees felt their choices were more constrained because of inequitable access
30 to high-status universities, discrimination at the point of entry or self-limiting choices for fear of being in a minority.
The research also found that young Muslims felt their transition into the labour market is then hampered by discrimination in the recruitment process. Once in work, young Muslims said racism, discrimination and lack of cultural awareness in the workplace had impacted on
35 their career development. Muslim women also felt that wearing the headscarf at work was an additional visual marker of difference that led to further discrimination.
The research suggested that many of these issues were worse for women. Within some communities, young Muslims felt that there are different expectations for boys and girls concerning their educational and employment outcomes, with boys having more freedom.
40 Within some communities, women are encouraged to focus on marriage and motherhood rather than to gain employment.

Workshop 1

→ students' book, pages 20/21

b Explain the underlined phrases in the report in your own words.

1 hate crimes _____
2 social mobility _____
3 work ethic _____
4 high resilience _____
5 stereotypical expectations _____
6 tailored support _____
7 inequitable access _____
8 self-limiting choices _____

c Classify the underlined phrases according to their connotations.

Positive connotation	Negative connotation	Both

13 VIEWING FOCUS: Young activists

a Saara Chaudry attended UNICEF Canada's Youth Activism Summit in Toronto in November 2019. She spoke to young activists about their experiences. Watch the video. What do these activists campaign for?

1 Rayne Fisher-Quann: _____
2 Abram Ilcisin: _____
3 Habon Ali: _____
4 Samantha Walsh: _____

b Watch the video again and do the tasks.

1 Describe how Rayne and Abram made their campaigns work.

_____
_____

2 Outline what advice Habon gives to young people.

_____
_____

3 Explain how, according to Samantha, you can become an activist.

_____
_____

14 fourteen

Workshop 1

students' book, pages 20/21

14 COP27

a Watch Sophia Kianni giving her speech at COP27 in 2022 and do the tasks.

1 Write down how Sophia reports Vanessa Nakate's words.

_____

_____

_____

2 Outline Sophia's main argument. Explain how she supports her argument.

_____

_____

3 Find examples of how she makes her speech persuasive.

_____

_____

b Report Sophia's words.

1 There is still not a single country that has a climate commitment compatible with 1.5.

She claimed _____

_____

2 Over 7 million people are dying prematurely every single year from breathing toxic air from the burning of fossil fuels.

She pointed out _____

_____

3 If the world took the action to meet WHO air quality guidelines, we would save millions of lives.

She said _____

_____

4 World leaders keep making excuses for not taking action.

She insisted _____

_____

5 What language do we need to translate the climate data into for you to take action?

Sophia asked _____

_____

Recognizing text types

15 Teach peace. Read the text and do the tasks.

1 Say where you think you would find this text.
2 Describe what sort of text it is. List its features.
3 Explain the aim of the text.

Join and Endorse the Campaign!

Join the Campaign today and help us #TeachPeace

Click here to submit your endorsement!

Show your commitment to support the goals of the Global Campaign to Teach Peace in Schools:
- build public awareness and support for the introduction of peace education in all schools throughout the world
- promote the education of all teachers and students to teach for peace.

When joining, please consider getting involved!

Get Involved

Volunteer list: join this list if you are interested in hearing about volunteer opportunities to support the campaign.
Country Coordinator: join this list if you are interested in starting up a country chapter of the campaign – or if you are interested in organizing support of the campaign in your world region.

Stay Connected

Choose your communication options and update anytime! Join and receive our monthly newsletter! It's full of news, analyses, events, and reports from around the globe.

Posts as they happen!
Receive a daily summary of new postings as they come hot off the press!
Receive a weekly overview of news, reviews & events!
Receive action alerts about time-sensitive campaigns and funding opportunities!

---

16 Your campaign. Think of a cause you would like to campaign for. You can look at the campaigns supported by the young activists you learned about in this Workshop for inspiration.

- Decide what cause you want to campaign for.
- Think about how you might persuade people to join your cause.
- Find an appropriate photo or design a logo.
- Think of a catchy title and indicate the purpose of your campaign clearly.
- Present your leaflet and campaign to the class.

Slum life

17 A rich country with a poor population

a Read this extract from an article about India's economy. Then complete it with the gerund or infinitive of the verbs in brackets.

This year, India's economy is expected _____ (1) (grow) by 7%, making it the fifth largest in the world, the International Monetary Fund (IMF) says. India's GDP is likely _____ (2) (rise) to around 3.5 trillion dollars. However, the sum spent on public healthcare ranks among the lowest in the world. In place of a well-funded public health service, the Indian government has only succeeded in _____ (3) (promote) an increasingly powerful commercial health sector. As a result, decent healthcare is a luxury only available to those who can afford _____ (4) (pay) for it. Despite _____ (5) (be) a top destination for medical tourism, India's poorest states have infant mortality rates higher than those in sub-Saharan Africa. In Bihar, eastern India, the public health service tries _____ (6) (address) the issues, but there aren't enough health centres to serve everyone, and the facilities that exist are ill equipped and understaffed. Minister Nitin Gadkari says that, even as India has emerged as the world's fifth largest economy, it continues _____ (7) (suffer) from starvation, unemployment, casteism, untouchability and inflation. Even though the government has promised _____ (8) (tackle) these issues and drive positive change, the minister admitted still _____ (9) (be) very far from this objective. The government plans _____ (10) (speed up) their efforts by _____ (11) (work) together and, of course, by not forgetting _____ (12) (care for) the poorest people in the country.

b Read the extract again and do the tasks.

1 Explain why the author establishes a relationship between the taxes the wealthiest pay in India and public spending on healthcare.
2 List the main issues that make Indian society so unequal.
3 Look for information about GDP and mortality rates in your country and compare them with India's.

Workshop 1

→ students' book, pages 24/25

18 **The need for water.** Listen to the podcast about water scarcity and do the tasks.

1. Describe the impact the lack of running water has on Chaya's health and on the relationships between village women and men.
2. Explain the significance of these figures: 17% – 4% – 74% – 65% – 2030.
3. Describe the impact of the monsoon season.
4. List the projects carried out by the Indian government and the World Bank on National Hydrology Projects.
5. Summarize the project in Pachvad village and describe one of the biggest challenges they faced.

19 How it began

a Read this summary of an interview with Krishna Pujari and answer the questions.

> In a recent interview, Krishna Pujari, co-founder of Reality Tours and Travel, discussed his journey as a social entrepreneur offering tours around various places in India, including Dhavari, one of Asia's biggest slums. Krishna explained that he moved to Mumbai at a young age and worked in various establishments before meeting his business partner,
> 5 Chris. Initially hesitant about foreigners, Krishna's friendship with Chris changed his perspective. Chris had previously volunteered in a school and later took tours of favelas in Brazil, which inspired the idea of conducting similar tours in Mumbai's Dharavi, home to more than half of Mumbai's population.
> Despite initial reservations, Krishna and Chris conducted extensive research and engaged
> 10 with the community before launching the concept. Krishna recalled facing scepticism from friends, who questioned their decision to take people on tours of the slums. Nonetheless, their determination led to the establishment of Reality Tours and Travel, offering a unique perspective and creating awareness of the reality of life in the slums.

1. What sets Dharavi apart from other places in Mumbai? _____
2. How did Krishna's perception of foreigners change after meeting Chris? _____
   _____
3. What experience did Chris base his proposal for Mumbai on? _____
   _____
4. What did the young entrepreneurs do? _____
   _____

b With a partner, list the pros and cons of slum tours.

- ☐ brings money into the local community
- ☐ creates jobs for tour guides
- ☐ encourages understanding of the underprivileged
- ☐ exploitation of slum residents and workers
- ☐ tours do not portray authentic situation
- ☐ profits largely go to tour operators
- ☐ promotes respect for enterprising workers
- ☐ genuine understanding impossible to achieve

Workshop 1

→ students' book, pages 26/27

@ WES-40346-001

Practice: Films about India

20 ***Slumdog Millionaire.*** Listen to the study notes about Salim and do the tasks.

1. Describe what events lead Salim to embrace a life of crime.
2. Comment on the relationship between Salim and Jamal.

21 **The film of the book**

a. Kamila and Bart are in the same Film Studies class. They have to compare films based on books. Listen to the first part of their conversation about *Slumdog Millionaire* and *Lion*. What makes this a good comparison, according to Kamila?

b. Listen to rest of their conversation and circle the correct answer.

1. Who has seen both films and read both books?   *Kamila | Bart | neither of them*
2. Why does Bart prefer *Lion* to *Slumdog Millionaire*?   *it's cool | fascinating | true*
3. Whose acting impresses Bart most?   *the women's | the men's | the children's*
4. What is Kamila's main criticism of the films?   *too boring | romantic | violent*

22 ***A passage to India:*** **film reviews**

a. Read extracts from two reviews of *A Passage to India*, the 1984 film written and directed by British director Sir David Lean, based on the novel by E. M. Forster. Complete each review with the letters A – F for the phrases given.

A meticulous craftsman
B perfectly modulated, quietly tension-filled
C that happens off stage
D that question equally open
E translate well to the screen
F unflashy performances

Review A

Great novels do not usually _____ (1). They are too filled with ambiguities, and movies have a way of making all their images seem like literal fact. *A Passage to India* is especially tricky, because the central event in the novel is something _____ (2), or never happens at all. In Forster's novel, it is never clear exactly what happened to Miss Quested after she
⁵ wandered alone into one of the caves. David Lean's film leaves _____ (3). But because he is dealing with a visual medium, he cannot make a mystery out of where Dr Aziz is at the time. So, in the film we know, or think we know, that Dr Aziz is innocent of the charges later brought against him. The charges and the trial fill the second half of the film, and Lean brings us to that point by a series of _____ (4) scenes.
¹⁰ Lean places the characters in one of the most beautiful canvases he has ever drawn. He makes India look like an amazing, beautiful place that an Englishman can never quite put his finger on. David Lean is a _____ (5), famous for going to any lengths to make every shot look just the way he thinks it should. His actors here are encouraged to give sound, thoughtful, _____ (6), and his screenplay is a model of clarity.

A didn't deserve to be nominated
B highly regarded film
C is more admirable
D predictable plot
E issues of racism and segregation
F the hightlight of the film

Review B
David Lean's _____ (1) *A Passage to India* was nominated for a whopping eleven Academy Awards, including Best Picture. Yet what makes this film so unusual is that it really _____ (2) for anything at all. It's excruciatingly interminable, long-winded, and meandering. And while the political and racial tensions of colonial India provide a unique backdrop to the _____ (3), the uninspiring manner in which it all unfolds is unforgivable.
The film won all eleven Oscar nominations including Best Director, Adapted Screenplay and Editing, all for David Lean. For a film that received so much praise, *A Passage to India* is terribly conventional. The acting is questionable at times, especially from Victor Banerjee, who plays Dr Aziz in such an over-the-top manner that it's difficult to take the forced naivety seriously. Judy Davis _____ (4) as Miss Quested, but her character is so despicable that focusing on her talent is not a dominant concern. Many scenes are devoted to portraying the Indians as mysterious and culturally unexplainable, while _____ (5) are ever-present in the political turmoil that displays the misunderstandings and bull-headed beliefs of the British leaders. As _____ (6), Professor Godbole (Alec Guinness, in a wonderfully comedic role) passes riddles of wisdom from person to person; but by the foreseeable conclusion, it's too late to save the project from its place amongst well-intentioned, immensely mediocre movie-making.

b Think of a film that you have seen which is based on a novel. Look for the description of a character and compare it to the film version. How similar or different are they?

_____
_____
_____
_____
_____
_____
_____
_____
_____
_____
_____
_____
_____
_____

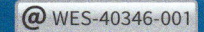

23 READING FOCUS: *A Passage to India:* the novel

a Read a review of the 1924 classic novel by E.M. Forster and complete it with the gerund or infinitive form of the verbs in brackets.

A Passage to India focuses on a relationship between a British schoolteacher and a Muslim doctor, reflecting **the larger tragedy of imperialism**. Today, the novel is considered to be **a timeless achievement** – one of the great novels of the 20th century. [...]
In January 1913, E. M. Forster visited the caves of Barabar on his first visit to India. He was deeply impressed and did not hesitate _____ (1) (*feature*) them as the Marabar caves in the central and all-important section of his masterpiece. [...]
The tortuous romantic drama of the Marabar caves is probably the part of *A Passage to India* that most readers are likely _____ (2) (*remember*). Adela Quested, an English schoolteacher, and her companion Mrs Moore arrive in Chandrapore and enter colonial India, a place obsessed with _____ (3) (*promote*) British values and the British way of life. Adela is expected _____ (4) (*marry*) Mrs Moore's son Ronny, an **eligible British civil servant**, and the city's magistrate. But she tries _____ (5) (*escape*) the prejudice of the British community and dreams of _____ (6) (*discover*) the 'real' India. She is assisted by Dr Aziz, a young well-respected Muslim doctor who keeps _____ (7) (*encourage*) **an entente** between the British and their colonial subjects. [...]
Aziz arranges for Adela and Mrs Moore _____ (8) (*visit*) the caves, but something happens that disgraces the doctor and **inflames the furious hostility** of the British. In the crisis, Aziz is imprisoned. [...] The head of the police regards the Indian character as _____ (9) (*be*) **inherently flawed** by an ingrained criminality. There appears _____ (10) (*be*) little doubt that Aziz will be found guilty because the word of an English woman is believed over the word of an Indian. Eventually, Adela **withdraws her charges** and Aziz, radicalized and angry, moves to the native state of Forster's imagination. 'I am an Indian at last,' he says. [...]

Source (abbreviated and adapted): Robert McCrum, "The 100 best novels: No 48 – A Passage to India by EM Forster (1924)", The Guardian, 18 August 2014, https://www.theguardian.com/books/2014/aug/18/100-best-novels-a-passage-to-india-em-forster-robert-mccrum [29.08.2023]

b Read the phrases in **bold** and explain what the writer means.

c Speculate about what might happen between Dr Aziz and Miss Quested and why this incident 'inflamed the hostility of the British'.

Traditional and modern cultures

24 Young Indian bloggers

a Complete this entry from Jasmina's blog with the correct form of the verbs from the box.

> ask (2x) ■ be (4x) ■ feel ■ have ■ ignore ■ say (2x) ■ tell

Indian culture has incorporated a variety of traditions and customs for hundreds of years and, even today, the values and norms of Indian culture play a significant role in Indian society. This _____ (1) especially true for a woman because we have to obey more stringent rules.

I was born, raised and educated in Germany, but the values and norms of Indian culture and Hinduism have always been important to my parents. For me, both cultures are a part of my identity, and both cultures enrich my life a lot. If you _____ (2) me about my personal values and standards, then I _____ (3) I tend more to my Indian side. I know that if I _____ (4) those values, I _____ (5) that I was denying my origins.

Every second year, I spend the summer holidays with my family in Chennai visiting our relatives because my parents do not want us to forget our roots. I think that has also contributed a lot to my own values.

Although I have traditional values, people in India still treat me as if I were a tourist. If I _____ (6) a conversation with young people, they _____ (7) usually shocked by my traditional views. If you _____ (8) any of my friends in India what young Europeans do, they _____ (9) you that they go to parties, drink a lot of alcohol, smoke cigarettes and have many relationships. This _____ (10) the image people from India have in their minds if you _____ (11) that you _____ (12) born and raised abroad.

My friends in India told me it has become normal in big cities for people to be in relationships and live out their love lives in public. It is not that the Indian traditions do not mean anything to them, but they find the Western way of life more attractive. There are still many young adults who strictly follow the rules of Indian culture. But it's interesting that, in a country where so many established taboos exist, young people are starting to break those rules.

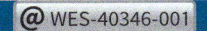

b Read the blogpost again and summarize the main points Jasmina makes (100 words).

c Choose the correct verbs to complete Aisha's blog.

I am a young Pakistani girl and I have lived most of my life in Germany. My father is very strict. If I **wear / would wear** (1) jeans or shorts in summer, he gets really mad. I'm invited to a party next week, but I'm sure I **won't be allowed to / am not allowed to** (2) go unless my aunt **will come / comes** (3) with me. And I certainly won't be able to go if I **uncover / would uncover** (4) my hair. My biggest worry is that, unless something **will change / changes** (5), I **will have to / have to** (6) marry someone I haven't chosen myself, just like my big sister did. **If / Unless** (7) I don't accept my father's choice of husband, he **sends / will send** (8) me to Pakistan where I don't know anyone. What would you do if you **were / would be** (9) me? Please send me a comment **when / if** (10) you have any advice.

25 **Indian etiquette.** Read these Indian etiquette rules and complete them with words and phrases from the box.

> are ■ can be minimized ■ go ■ if ■ it is ■ know ■ unless ■ visited ■ wanted ■ will probably feel ■ won't see ■ would also be ■ would be ■ would you do ■ you needed ■ you visit

- If _____ (1) India for the very first time, you _____ (2) a bit apprehensive, not knowing what to expect. The culture shock _____ (3) somewhat if you _____ (4) beforehand what to expect.

- You definitely _____ (5) a well-dressed Indian man wearing shorts, or an Indian woman wearing a skirt above the ankles _____ (6) you _____ (7) at the beach in Goa.

- A woman can't go into a temple with her legs, shoulders or head uncovered. If a European woman _____ (8) to go into a temple in shorts or a short skirt, she _____ (9) asked to leave.

- If you _____ (10) into someone's home, _____ (11) good manners to take your shoes off. And that _____ (12) a prerequisite _____ (13) you _____ (14) a temple or a mosque.

- Pointing with your finger is rude in India. So, what _____ (15) if _____ (16) to point at something or someone? It's better to do it with your whole hand or thumb.

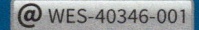

Practice: Sounds of India

26 Musical discoveries

a Listen to a conversation between Emil and Theo and do the tasks.

1. Say which instruments are mentioned in the conversation.
2. List the countries Emil mentions.
3. Say what instrument Emil is playing and the information he gives about it.
4. Describe how he became interested in Indian music and in this instrument.
5. Explain the role a teacher played in this.

b Listen again and write down the conditional sentences that Emil uses. Say what type they are and why Emil uses a different type in each case.

27 Ravi Shankar

a After his conversation with Emil, Theo read Ravi Shankar's bio. Read the text and complete it with the letters A – F for the phrases below.

A gaining worldwide recognition as a master of North Indian classical music
B the guidance of a renowned teacher named Allauddin Khan
C while Shankar gained newfound fame as a mentor to the so-called 'Quiet Beatle'
D introduced traditional Indian music to a wider American audience
E embraced the opportunity to learn from Shankar
F came together in friendship and solidarity

Born in 1920 in Benares, India, Ravi Shankar's early years were spent touring India and Europe as a dancer with his brother's troupe. However, he later shifted his focus to studying the sitar under _____ (1). After completing his training, Shankar pursued a career as a composer _____ (2). His influence extended far and inspired musicians both in India and abroad.

During the 1950s, Shankar embarked on a mission to introduce Indian music to the global stage, traveling extensively to the United States and Western Europe. His traditional Indian attire and music left a lasting impression on audiences during this time.

A significant turning point occurred in 1966 when Shankar crossed paths with George Harrison, a prominent rock musician. Harrison, already a fan of the sitar, _____ (3). This marked the beginning of a close friendship and collaboration between the two artists. Harrison tried to learn as much as possible about Indian culture and spirituality during his time with Shankar, _____ (4).

continued on page 25

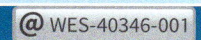

The partnership also opened doors for
Shankar, making him a popular performer at festivals and television shows. His performance at the 1967 Monterey Pop Festival _____ (5).

In 1971, Shankar and Harrison collaborated once again, organizing a benefit concert for the people of Bangladesh who were suffering from a time of famine and war. Shankar played an important role in the success of 'The Concert for Bangladesh', showcasing his commitment to humanitarian causes.

Despite their different backgrounds, George Harrison and Ravi Shankar _____ (6), using their talents and passion for music to help those in need.

b Read the text again and do the tasks.

1 Describe how Shankar's relationship with George Harrison helped him become famous and respected.

_____
_____
_____

2 Interpret the following statement: 'His traditional Indian attire and music left a lasting impression on audiences during this time.'

_____
_____
_____

3 Research and present other famous musicians who have used their talent to help those less fortunate.

_____
_____
_____

Workshop 1

→ students' book, pages 30/31

28 **SPEAKING FOCUS:** *In Her Name*

a Do some research on Anoushka Shankar's and her music.

b Watch the music video *In her name*, concentrating on the middle part (02:40 – 04:40). What is the theme? What makes you say that?

c Describe your reaction to the video. Why do you think Shankar decided to make it? Discuss your ideas with a partner.

29 **Theo's thoughts**

a Read Theo's conversation with Amara about Anoushka Shankar and answer the questions.

A I didn't know you were interested in the music of India!
T Well, it's all Emil's fault. I heard him playing the sitar the other day and he told me about Ravi and Anoushka Shankar. I started looking and I've discovered I love the music! I like Ravi Shankar, but I think Anoushka is amazing.
5 A I'm a huge fan, too. Not only because of her music, but also because of her activism. She's using her music to reflect her support of women's rights and social justice. Have you seen the video *In her name*?
T I don't think so. What's it about?
A She used a song she had recorded some years ago to accompany a poem. It's her personal
10 response to the horrific gang-rape of Jyoti Singh Pandey in Delhi in 2011. If you check her out on social media, you will learn more about it. She explains that she also recorded the video to tell her own story of abuse. Her 2019 album, *Land of Gold*, originated in the context of the humanitarian crisis of refugees in the US and it explores their stories with 11 original compositions featuring female activist hip-hop star M.I.A.
15 T I'm going to look for the video and the album. She is truly amazing!

1 Why did Shankar record the video? What personal experience does Amara mention?
2 How does this new information affect your initial reaction to the video?
3 What is the theme of Shankar's latest album? Why do you think she called it *Land of Gold*?

b Now read Theo's comments about Anoushka Shankar and complete them with the correct form of the verbs in the box.

> agree ■ ask ■ be ■ come ■ love ■ organize

1 If Anoushka Shankar gave a concert here, I _____ it.
2 Will you let me know if she _____ to Germany?
3 It _____ fantastic if I could meet her!
4 I _____ our music teacher if she can lend me a sitar.
5 Do you think she _____ to come to our school if we invited her?
6 If I _____ a charity festival to support refugees, would you help me?

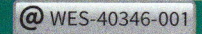

Preparing to write a text

30 Gender equality

a Read the first and last paragraphs of an article on campaigning for gender equality. Then, order the other paragraphs to complete the full article.

1 Gender equality is a pressing issue today, as our society continues to believe in and act upon stereotypes and biases that propagate gender inequalities. The global fight for gender equality needs to be driven forward with renewed vigour and passion if we are to achieve a more equitable world for all.

7 We owe it to the victims who have felt the brunt of the oppressive, patriarchal system. We owe it to our children to ensure that they grow up in a world where gender does not constrain them. We owe it to ourselves to create a world that is more just and equitable for all. Remember, the fight for gender equality is our fight. Let us not turn away from it.

A So what form should this challenge take? It can involve campaigning and mobilizing communities around the issue, which could include organizing protest rallies, marches or other public events to draw attention to the issue. It is also important to make sure gender equality issues are discussed in the media and other public forums. Campaigning can be done through advocacy, lobbying and public education. Advocacy involves making sure public institutions and services are aware of and responsive to gender equality concerns. This can be done through petitions, press releases and other forms of public outreach. Lobbying involves pressuring politicians and policymakers to create and pass legislation that will promote gender equality. And public education involves raising awareness about gender equality and its importance.

B However, it is important to be mindful of the different experiences people have and to be respectful of all genders. It is also important to be aware of the power dynamics.

C It is important to start by looking at the world through a gendered lens and to recognize the distinct and separate experiences of men and women. We must acknowledge the multiple dimensions of gender inequality that exist. And we must challenge existing gender roles and promote true gender equality.

D Many defend the status quo, often arguing that gender roles in our society are natural. But this natural argument belittles and ignores the daily struggles and marginalization of many women. We must be reminded of the wage gap between men and women, which may be as wide as 25%, and the staggering number of women globally who are victims of violence and lack education as a result of structural inequalities.

b Find examples of the following: *counterarguments, emotive language, examples, facts, repetition, rhetorical questions, statistics, warnings.*

31 **Raising awareness.** Choose a cause you feel strongly about and write an article for the school blog or a magazine for teenagers (150 words). Anticipate the counter arguments and write the article trying to persuade your audience and raise awareness of the issue.

Mediation

32 **What's love got to do with it?**

a You and your classmates are working on a poster project about third generation immigrants in the UK. You have been asked to provide information about a film about arranged marriages. You found this German review. Prepare a text in English (150 words) summing up what the story is and what the reviewer thinks about it.

WHAT'S LOVE GOT TO DO WITH IT? (2023)
Eine Filmkritik von Markus Fiedler

WIE LUSTIG IST EINE ARRANGIERTE HEIRAT? Komödien, in denen es um kulturelle Unterschiede geht, erweisen sich seit vielen Jahren regelmäßig als Hits in den Kinos. [...] „What's Love Got To Do With It"
5 schlägt in diese Kerbe und beschäftigt sich mit den arrangierten Hochzeiten, die in vielen Familien mit indischen oder pakistanischen Wurzeln in England noch immer eine Rolle spielen. Denn der aus einer pakistanischen Familie stammende Arzt Kazim möchte
10 nach einigen Enttäuschungen seine Eltern für ihn nach einer Braut suchen lassen. Und seine Nachbarin und beste Freundin aus Kindertagen, die Dokumentarfilmerin Zoe, ist stets mit der Kamera dabei, um das Geschehen einzufangen und einen Film daraus zu machen.

15 Dass natürlich alles anders kommt, als Kazim und Zoe sich das so überlegt haben, liegt bei einer Rom-Com in der Natur der Sache. Allerdings haben sich Drehbuchautorin Jemima Khan und der indische Regisseur Shekhar Kapur, [...], mit der arrangierten Ehe nicht unbedingt ein klassisches Thema für eine Komödie ausgesucht. Schließlich steht diese Form der Eheschließung vor allem in streng muslimischen Ländern immer wieder
20 in der Kritik von Menschenrechtsorganisationen, die sowohl Kinderehen als auch die starke Einschränkung der Selbstbestimmung von Frauen anprangern.
Um dennoch für Lacher zu sorgen, muss das sensible Thema dementsprechend weichgespült werden. Und so bleibt bei „What's Love Got To Do With It" die Kritik am traditionellen System eher ein Feigenblatt, als dass hier ein differenziertes Bild
25 gezeichnet würde. [...]
Denn natürlich geht es im Kern um die Beziehung zwischen Kazim und Zoe, die sich schon so lange kennen, dass sie einander als möglichen Partner ausschließen – bis es eigentlich zu spät ist. Wenn das Ende eines Films schon keinerlei Überraschung beinhaltet, dann sollte zumindest der Weg dorthin mit der einen oder anderen
30 originellen Idee gepflastert sein. Das gelingt Kapur und Khan nur bedingt. Zwar herrscht an sympathischen Figuren kein Mangel, so kann Emma Thompson als Zoes alleinstehende Mutter in jeder Szene begeistern und steuert einen großen Teil der besten Lacher im Film bei. Frisch ist dieser Charakter aber ebenso wenig wie die ganze Familie Kazims, die mit allerlei erwartbaren Klischees in keinem Moment etwas Neues
35 zu bieten hat.
Umso wichtiger ist es, dass nicht nur die berühmte Chemie zwischen den Figuren stimmt, sondern die auch mit ihrem Charme das Publikum jederzeit abholen. Und hier

kann Kapurs Film tatsächlich liefern. Lily James fungiert hier einmal mehr als fleischgewordene Niedlichkeit [...]. Filmpartner Shazad Latif harmoniert mit James auf
⁴⁰ eine burschikose Art, die die Freundschaft seit Kindertagen glaubhaft erscheinen lässt. Dazu passt die britische Kleinfamilie aus Mutter und Tochter gut zur pakistanischen Großfamilie nebenan, die enge Freundschaft wirkt in keinem Moment aufgesetzt oder unecht.
Dank dieser Zutaten können Rom-Com-Fans, [...], hier bedenkenlos das Kinoticket
⁴⁵ kaufen. Auch wenn, bei Licht betrachtet, die Komödie für ihre Thematik deutlich zu harmlos ausfällt und zugunsten der Wohlfühl-Atmosphäre durchaus denkbare Spitzen weglässt. [...]

Source (abbreviated): Markus Fiedler, "What's love got to do with it? (2023) – Wie lustig ist eine arrangierte Heirat?", Kino-Zeit, https://www.kino-zeit.de/film-kritiken-trailer-streaming/whats-love-got-to-do-with-it-2023 [29.08.2023]

b After you have written your text, a friend asks you how the film was received in Britain. You do some research and find a lot of positive reviews but also a few negative ones. Look at these two negative reviews and explain them to your friend in German. What is the main concern of the reviewers?

Amana B. ☆

From the promo and the trailer, I had very high expectations, but the complete film is rubbish. Even the music isn't fitting. The dialogues are poor, the actors wooden, Emma Thompson is a caricature. But what annoyed me most is the way our Muslim culture was presented. Nothing in the film highlights anything good about our culture. No mention of the positive values, of closely-knit families, of respect for our elders. The makers of this film are absolutely clueless.

KZK ☆☆

I tried to like this film, also because Jemima Khan is usually such a staunch supporter of Pakistani culture. But this time she got it wrong. She has done exactly the opposite to what she claims to have portrayed in this film. She believes that this is a fair portrayal of Muslims and Pakistan. But all she is doing is reinforcing boring narratives and cultural and religious stereotypes about POCs* (in this case particularly Pakistanis and/or Muslims). So, my message to her and white directors elsewhere is, please try not to steal our narrative. Do your research properly or leave the film-making to us POCs.

* People of Colour

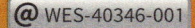

My review

1 About India and Pakistan
1. was granted
2. was partitioned
3. had been raised
4. were ignored
5. was ruled
6. was finally achieved
7. had been anounced
8. is viewed
9. are thought
10. has been estimated
11. were torn apart
12. has been felt
13. has not been achieved
14. cannot be described
15. are frequently suspected
16. are considered

2 About climate matters
1. Rani said that she had joined the Green Youth Movement after the devastating floods they had experienced.
2. She also added that she intended to follow in the footsteps of Licypriya Kangujam who'd been a youth activist since she was four years old.
3. Jai pointed out that they needed to focus on issues that mattered to everyone, such as education and health.
4. Kavi emphasized that their education system needed to change to give equal opportunities to girls.
5. Neel stated that he wanted to raise awareness of the extensive use of plastic.
6. Ajay mentioned that he had joined a march demanding that CO_2 emissions were lowered as the air pollution in Delhi was too high.
7. Arun wondered whether there was anything more effective than collaborating with international environmental organizations.
8. Vin added that she had realized how important social media was in reaching like-minded activists.
9. Uma told the others that she had been following Malala's story, for her she was a real inspiration.
10. Devi asked what hope there was for their generation if young people didn't act together.

3 About Indian slums
1. wondering
2. to let
3. making
4. to get on with
5. looking for / to look for
6. to come up with
7. to find
8. to pass
9. living
10. being

4 About traditions and cultures

a
1. marry
2. asked
3. will listen
4. does not accept
5. would do
6. need

b
1. lived
2. had
3. told
4. will find
5. was not
6. ordered
7. lived
8. would be

Hi from Jozi!

1 How it all started. Read the transcript from a radio programme about South African history and complete it with the words in the box.

> ancestors ■ anchoring ■ exploration ■ fossils ■
> inhabited ■ migrated ■ monument ■ trading

For over 100,000 years, humans have lived in the southern tip of Africa, and their hominid _____ (1) for about 3.5 million years. The Cradle of Humankind, recognized as a UNESCO World Heritage Site near Johannesburg, holds the oldest and biggest collection of hominid _____ (2), some dating back 3.5
5 million years. Homo sapiens, our species, have _____ (3) this region for at least 170,000 years.

Bantu-speaking groups, skilled in farming and iron smelting, _____ (4) south from Central Africa about 3,000 years ago. By 500 AD, they had reached the eastern part of South Africa, becoming ancestors to present-day Zulu people and other groups.
10 European interaction with the region started with Portuguese _____ (5) in the late 1400s. They were looking for a sea route around the Cape of Good Hope to reach their Indian _____ (6) posts. This sea route was dominated by the Portuguese in the 15th century. Bartolomeu Dias, in his Cape exploration, erected three crosses and stone pillars, including the oldest _____ (7)
15 in South Africa at Kwaaihoek. Vasco da Gama ultimately established the sea route to India, _____ (8) at what is now Durban Harbour on Christmas Day 1497, creating a significant port on the African continent.

2 The 17th and 18th centuries. Listen to the second part of the programme and do the quiz.

1. When was a colony in Table Bay established?
   ☐ 1652 ☐ 1658 ☐ 1795 ☐ 1862

2. In what year did Dutch settlers start to migrate north?
   ☐ 1795 ☐ 1815 ☐ 1818 ☐ 1836

3. When was gold discovered in Witwatersrand?
   ☐ 1795 ☐ 1867 ☐ 1815 ☐ 1884

4. When did the Anglo-Boer War break out?
   ☐ 1898 ☐ 1899 ☐ 1902 ☐ 1910

5. When did South Africa become fully independent from the British Parliament?
   ☐ 1898 ☐ 1910 ☐ 1931 ☐ 1948

6. In which year was apartheid formalized in a series of laws?
   ☐ 1898 ☐ 1899 ☐ 1931 ☐ 1948

thirty-one 31

3 Multilingual South Africa. Complete the text with words in the box and put the verbs in brackets in the correct form.

> although ■ as well as ■ both ■ each ■ however ■ such as

South Africa is an incredibly diverse country, _____ (1) culturally and linguistically. Altogether, there are eleven official languages in South Africa, _____ (2) _____ (3) (*represent*) a specific cultural group or community within the country. The most widely spoken language is IsiZulu, used by around 22% of the population. Other major languages in South Africa _____ (4) (*include*) IsiXhosa (16%), Sepedi (9%), Setswana (8%), Sesotho (7%), English (7%), Xitsonga (4%), Afrikaans (4%) and Venda (4%). English is the lingua franca of South Africa and _____ (5) (*use*) mainly for business and government communication. _____ (6), most of the population is multilingual, and many people _____ (7) (*be able to*) speak several languages. Multilingualism is one of the many aspects that makes South Africa a unique and vibrant country. South Africa is also home to many minority languages, _____ (8) German, Greek and Gujarati, which _____ (9) (*speak*) by small minority groups. _____ (10) these languages do not have official status, they play an important role in the cultural identity of South Africa. The eleven official languages of South Africa _____ (11) (*protect*) by the constitution, and the government _____ (12) (*put*) in place measures _____ (13) (*promote*) the use and understanding of these languages.

Practice: Accept and respect

4 **Winnie Mandela.** Read this text about Winnie Mandela and do the tasks on page 34.

Winnie Mandela was the former wife of South African President Nelson Mandela and former leader of the African National Congress (ANC) Women's League. Born in the village of Mbongweni in South Africa's Eastern Cape Province in 1936,
5 Mandela travelled throughout South Africa during her youth and managed to attend school despite strict apartheid measures. She earned a degree in social work [...], and despite the opportunity to continue her studies in America, accepted a position as a social worker at the Baragwanath Hospital in
10 Johannesburg, where she was the first qualified black medical social worker. She eventually studied at the University of Witwatersrand, and earned a bachelor's degree in international relations.
Much of Mandela's interest in racial politics began while she
15 served at the hospital and conducted research into infant mortality rates in the nearby Alexandra Townships. She met her future husband Nelson Mandela in 1957 while he was standing trial for treason because of his civil disobedience campaigns in the early 1950s. The two were married in 1958, and their daughters Zenani and Zinzi were born in 1959 and 1960, respectively. They lived only four years as a
20 married couple because beginning in 1962, Nelson Mandela was imprisoned for 27 years, spending 18 of those years on Robben Island.
During her husband's imprisonment, the government restricted Winnie Mandela to the Orlando Township in Soweto. She was prevented from working but flouted this order and worked for the African National Congress (ANC). Beginning in 1969, she served seventeen
25 months in prison in solitary confinement, accused of various crimes under the Terrorism Act. Later, she was sentenced to house arrest. In 1976 [...], Mandela became one of the co-founders of the Black Women's Federation and the Black Parents' Association. [...] Mandela's increasingly radical views caused some anti-apartheid groups to distance themselves from her, despite her unofficial title as "Mother of the Nation." Her small
30 circle of bodyguards, nicknamed the Mandela United Football Club, was sometimes accused of cruelty and terrorism. The 1990s proved highly controversial for Mandela. She was present when her husband was released from prison in February 1990, but the two were separated in 1992 and divorced in 1996. [...]
In 1991, Winnie Mandela was elected to the executive board of the ANC. That same
35 year, she was charged and convicted, along with members of her Mandela United Football Club, with the kidnapping and murder of 14-year-old ANC activist Stompie Moeketsi. Despite this, she went on to be elected and serve ten years as the president of the ANC Women's League, from 1993 to 2003. She finally resigned after multiple accusations and convictions of fraud and theft.
40 Winnie Mandela returned to the South African Parliament in 2009. After a long illness, she died in a Johannesburg hospital on April 2, 2018. She was 81.

Source (abbreviated): Sarah Bartlett, Winnie Madikizela-Mandela (1936 – 2018), Black Past, 4 October 2010, https://www.blackpast.org/global-african-history/mandela-winnie-madikizela-1936/ [29.08.2023]

1 Characterize Winnie Mandela's role in the anti-apartheid movement.
2 Describe how her actions and views evolved over time and what influenced them.
3 Discuss the controversies surrounding Winnie Mandela's actions, including the accusations against her.
4 Explain why some anti-apartheid groups distanced themselves from Winnie Mandela.
5 Reflect on the impact of her life and work on South African history and society.

5 **The end of apartheid.** Complete this blogpost about Mandela and the end of apartheid with relative pronouns and *where* and *when*.

Originally, the use of civil resistance against apartheid was based on Gandhian ideas, _____ (1) used mostly legal tactics of protest. It originated in South Africa in 1906, _____ (2) it gained support among the many oppressed communities. Soon, the ANC, _____ (3) was founded in 1912, became a major force _____ (4) opposed the oppression of the 80% non-European population of the country. The ANC, _____ (5) tactics of protest during its first four decades had been mostly legal, became more militant in the early 1950s, _____ (6) it began using non-violent direct action.

White South Africans, _____ (7) deliberately excluded non-whites from economic and political power, developed an explicit theology and philosophy of white racial superiority, _____ (8) legal system monopolized control over the state and the economy. However, it became increasingly reliant upon non-white labour and isolated from international diplomacy and trading places, when its inequalities became evident. Discouraged by the lack of results from their non-violent campaign, Nelson Mandela and others, _____ (9) had created the Umkhonto We Sizwe (Spear of the Nation), called for an armed uprising. That, too, failed, but in the end, a concerted grassroots non-violent civil resistance movement in coalition with international support and sanctions forced the white government to negotiate.

On 17 March 1992, two-thirds of South Africa's white voters approved a negotiated end of the minority regime and the apartheid system. Free, all-race, national elections, were held in 1994 for the first time in South African history, resulting in a black majority government led by Nelson Mandela, _____ (10) became the first black president of the country.

Workshop 2

6 **VIEWING FOCUS:** *District 9*

a Watch the first part of the trailer for *District 9*. Discuss with a partner what you think the film is about. What makes you say that? Justify your answers.

b Now watch the second part of the trailer. Were your ideas correct? What does the film remind you of?

c Use the information in the box to write a review (100 words). Use relative pronouns and *when* and *where*.

> **Film:** *District 9* (2009, South Africa)
> **Director:** Neill Blomkamp; feature film debut for Blomkamp
> **Achievements:** received four Academy Awards nominations
> **Production:** produced by Peter Jackson; co-production involving New Zealand, the United States and South Africa
> **Cast:** stars South African actors: Sharlto Copley, Jason Cope, David James
> **Narrative Style:** partially presented in a found footage format; features fictional interviews, news footage, and surveillance camera videos
> **Setting:** story is set in Johannesburg, South Africa
> **Inspiration:** inspired by events in Cape Town's District Six during the apartheid era

Sports and politics

7 Sports and apartheid. Kenny, Annika and Elton are talking about sports during apartheid. Listen to their conversation and choose the correct answer(s) for each question.

1. What was the D'Oliveira Affair?
   - a A controversy over a cricket player from South Africa
   - b A controversy over a cricket player from England
   - c An uproar over South African apartheid laws

2. What was the outcome of this affair?
   - a The tour was cancelled.
   - b The tour was allowed to go ahead.
   - c The apartheid laws were lifted.

3. Who did South Africa ban?
   - a Athletes from other countries
   - b Non-white athletes
   - c Tennis players

4. What happened after the government rejected Arthur Ashe's visa applications three times?
   - a He gave up on his dream of competing in South Africa.
   - b He started protesting against the government.
   - c He began lobbying tennis governing bodies to take action against the South Africa Open.

5. What was the result of Arthur Ashe's lobbying efforts?
   - a The South Africa Open was cancelled.
   - b They contributed to the two-decade process of dismantling apartheid.
   - c He managed to play and win in Johannesburg.

8 Arthur Ashe's legacy

a Kenny did some research and found an article about Arthur Ashe's activism. Read the article and give each paragraph a title.

A _____

South Africa announced the rejection of Arthur Ashe's second visa application in January 1970, citing his 'general antagonism' towards the country. This led to anti-apartheid protests against South African
5 athletes around the world. Ashe could have given up, but instead he lobbied the tennis governing bodies to take action against the South Africa Open and called for South Africa's expulsion from the Davis Cup competition.

B _____

10 While the world's tennis organizations prepared to confront South Africa, Ashe travelled to Washington, D.C. to testify before a House Foreign Affairs subcommittee looking into potential action against South Africa. In response to a question about a possible reciprocal ban against South African athletes, Ashe said his 'moral conscience' had
15 told him this would solve nothing. 'I wouldn't want them to suffer the same indignities from my government that I have from theirs.'

Ashe in Wimbledon, 1968

C _____

However, Arthur Ashe had difficulty convincing his fellow tennis players, who were all white, to join him in protesting against South Africa's apartheid policy. Most of them were not interested in taking part in political activism. They opposed South Africa's decision, but believed that taking action would be ineffective.

D _____

In 1973, with South Africa facing considerable international political and economic pressure, Ashe was finally granted a visa for the South Africa Open, but he refused to play unless seating for his matches was unsegregated – but that was beyond even his star powers. White spectators watched him from up close, non-whites mostly from afar.

E _____

In 1974, one particular interaction left an impression on him that he could not shake. During the South African Open that year, there was a black child, about 14, who followed Ashe obsessively through the tournament grounds. When Ashe asked him why he did so, the boy told Ashe he was 'the first truly free black man' he had ever seen. Ashe devoted himself to speaking out against apartheid for the next 20 years, giving speeches about the issue, endorsing international sanctions against South Africa and encouraging other players not to play there. In 1985, he was arrested for protesting against apartheid in front of the South African Embassy in Washington, D.C.

Ashe watches while the singer and actor Harry Belafonte speaks at a news conference at the United Nations Headquarters to announce the formation of Artists and Athletes Against Apartheid.

b Complete these *if*-sentences type 3 with the correct form of the verbs in brackets.

1 Kenny might not have known about Arthur Ash if his grandparents _____ _____ (*not see*) him win at Wimbledon.

2 If Ashe hadn't been such a fan of South African tennis, he _____ _____ (*might not fight*) so hard to play there.

3 If he _____ (*give up*), the anti-apartheid protests against South African athletes might not have gained momentum.

4 He _____ (*might support*) a reciprocal ban against South African athletes if his moral conscience hadn't guided him.

5 Would Ashe's fight against South Africa's apartheid policy have been easier if his fellow tennis players _____ (*be interested*) in political activism?

6 If Arthur Ashe _____ (*not be inspired*) by the black child's words, he might not have dedicated so much of his time and energy to fighting against apartheid and advocating for change.

Workshop 2

@ WES-40346-002

→ students' book, pages 60/61

Practice: Headline news

9 **Stories of achievement.** Tricia has written a blogpost about South African female Paralympian athletes. Read it and choose the correct options to complete it.

Whether they were born with a disability or whether it was caused by a life-changing setback, the women of South Africa's Paralympian team have proved that despite their physical differences, their sporting triumph knows no bounds. [...] There's no doubt about
it. If they **had allowed / had been allowed / hadn't allowed** (1) their disabilities to define them, they **will live up / would live up / wouldn't have lived up** (2) to their utmost potential. By overcoming them, they have unquestionably become an inspiration to other differently-abled and able-bodied people alike. Here we have two examples.
Sandra Khumalo has made a name for herself in the world of sports. If she **had not had / didn't have / wouldn't have** (3) a car accident which left her lower body paralysed, she **might continue / may continue / might have continued** (4) working at a safari lodge in the Kruger National Park and she **might never have discovered / might discover / might have discovered** (5) her talent and passion for rowing.
Zanele Situ became paralysed from her fourth vertebra down when her spinal cord picked up a TB infection. If her teachers in Umtata **had not encouraged / did not encourage / had encouraged** (6) her to practise javelin, she **wouldn't have become / hadn't become / didn't become** (7) South Africa's first black woman to win a Paralympic gold medal. If she **wouldn't have worked / would have worked / hadn't worked** (8) so hard and **hadn't / hadn't had / didn't have** (9) the support of her family and coaches, she **would achieve / wouldn't achieve / wouldn't have achieved** (10) this.
If these women **had not embraced / didn't embrace / wouldn't embrace** (11) their disabilities, they **hadn't had / might have had / might not have had** (12) the opportunities they have today to showcase their talent and make a positive impact on the world. They have overcome obstacles and continue to be inspiring role models for everyone.

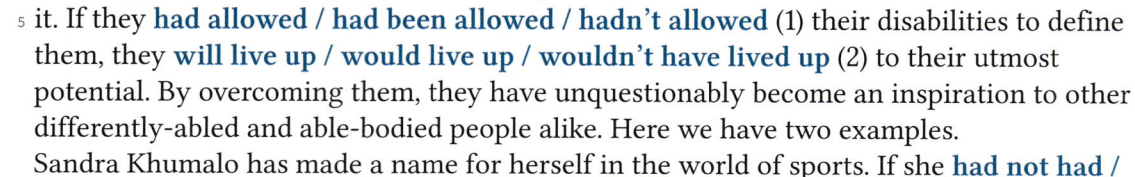

Source (abbreviated and adapted): Zeenat Mowzer, "10 SA female Paralympians who achieved glory despite the odds", news24, 18 September 2016, https://www.news24.com/life/archive/10-sa-female-paralympians-who-achieved-glory-despite-the-odds-20160918 [29.08.2023]

10 **Sports activism**

a Listen to a podcast about tennis activists, make notes and explain the importance of these women.

1. Venus and Serena Williams
2. Martina Navratilova
3. Billie Jean King

b Listen to the next episode of the podcast and do the tasks.

1. Outline Billie Jean King's sporting achievements.
2. Say why you think the match between B.J. King and Bobby Riggs was called the 'Battle of the Sexes'.
3. Summarize what the Women's Tennis Association and the Women's Sports Foundation are, and the role King played in them.

38 thirty-eight

11 READING FOCUS: Sports stars and controversies

a Read the headlines and decide whether they are positive or negative. Then read the article and choose the best headline (A–E) or write your own.

> **A** Sports Stars Take Centre Stage in Social Activism ■ **B** Sportspeople as Social Advocates: A Critique ■ **C** The Misguided Attempts of Athletes to Make a Difference ■ **D** The Power of Personal Experience: Athletes Bringing Attention to Social Issues ■ **E** The Dangers of Athletes Dabbling in Social Issues

_____

Sportspeople have long been seen as role models and leaders in society, and many use their influence to advocate for social issues. While sportspeople can bring significant attention to important causes, there are both positive and negative aspects to this kind of activism.

5 One of the most positive aspects of sportspeople advocating for social issues is that they can bring significant attention to these causes. With millions of followers on social media and the ability to reach millions more through their public appearances and interviews, sportspeople have a powerful platform to raise awareness of important issues. This kind of advocacy can lead to more resources being dedicated to tackling these problems and can inspire others to get involved.

10 Another positive aspect is that sportspeople can use their personal experiences to give a unique perspective on social issues. For example, an athlete who has experienced discrimination or prejudice first hand can use their own story to inspire change and bring attention to the importance of tackling these issues. This kind of personal connection to the cause can also inspire others to get involved.

However, there are also some negative aspects to sportspeople campaigning for social issues. One of
15 the biggest challenges is that some people may not take the cause seriously if it is being promoted by athletes. Some may see it as a publicity stunt or a way for athletes to boost their own profile, and this can undermine the message they want to convey and the impact they hope to have.

Another issue is that some sportspeople may not have the right skills or knowledge to effectively advocate for a cause, and thus make mistakes or miss important details, which can harm the cause and
20 their credibility. Additionally, some people may be sceptical of athletes who are suddenly taking a strong stance on a social issue, especially if they have not shown a strong commitment to the cause in the past.

In conclusion, there are both positive and negative aspects to sportspeople campaigning for social issues. While athletes can bring significant attention and inspiration to important causes, they also face challenges such as not being taken seriously and not having the right skills and knowledge to effectively
25 advocate for a cause. Ultimately, the impact that sportspeople have on social issues will depend on how they use their platform and how effectively they can communicate their message to the public.

b Read the article again and answer the questions.

1. How can athletes raise awareness for social causes?
2. What is one major positive outcome of sportspeople using their personal experiences to advocate for social issues?
3. How can a sportsperson's personal connection to a social cause enhance the effectiveness of their advocacy?
4. What challenge might arise when some people perceive athletes' involvement in social issues as a publicity stunt?
5. What negative consequences can occur if sportspeople lack the necessary skills or knowledge to effectively advocate for a social issue?

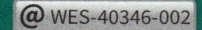

Analysing an extract

12 How to analyse an extract*

a Read the summary of a novel written in 1948 and Extract A and the notes. Then do the tasks.

> In Alan Paton's *Cry, the Beloved Country*, Zulu pastor Stephen Kumalo's journey to find his son in apartheid-era Johannesburg reveals a society torn by racial injustice. The novel delves into the stark contrasts of urban and rural life, portraying societal breakdown. Despite the bleakness, Paton's narrative ultimately holds a message of hope for societal healing and transformation.

Extract A: Kumalo and his wife have had bad news from Johannesburg.
[Kumalo] went out of the door, and she[1] watched him through the little window, walking slowly to the door of the church. Then she sat down at his table[2], and put her head on it, and was silent[3], with the patient suffering[4] of black women[5], with the suffering of oxen[6], with the suffering of any that are mute[7].

[1] no name: gender inequality, passivity
[2] their home has a table but it's not hers
[3] as a woman, has no voice
[4] situation of women, suffering
[5] disadvantaged by race and gender
[6] repetition; biblical reference of hardworking animal
[7] poetic for silent, unable to speak

1 Kumalo's wife is never named in the novel. Explain what this illustrates.
2 Describe how repetition is used to portray the woman, using quotes from the extract.

b Read Extract B and the notes. Then do the task.

Extract B: Kumalo is welcomed by friendly Anglican priests.
They went into a room where a table was laid[1], and there he met many priests, both white and black[2], and they sat down after grace and ate together[3]. He was a bit nervous of the many plates and knives and forks[4], but watched what the others did, and used the things likewise[5].

[1] contrast with simple rural life; a laid table remarkable
[2] very unusual for white and black men to sit together
[3] bonding by religious faith
[4] simple everyday objects are unknown to Kumalo
[5] poetic, biblical language; could have said 'did the same'

1 Describe how Paton evokes Kumalo's emotions as he dines with the other priests.
2 Explain what sets Kumalo apart from the others, and what binds him to them.

13 Annotate an extract. Discuss what the author wants to convey and how he does it.

> **Extract C:** *His son had gone astray in the great city, where so many others had gone astray before him, and where many others would go astray after him, until there was found some great secret that as yet no man had discovered. But that he should kill a man, a white man! There was nothing that he could remember, nothing, nothing at all, that could make it probable.*

*Extracts on this page: Alan Paton, *Cry, the Beloved Country*, Penguin Books, 1958. A: p. 11; B: p. 20; C: p. 77

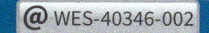

Wildlife in South Africa

14 South African game

a Complete an article Tricia is reading with letters A – N for the phrases below. Then give it a title.

A although South Africa is
B back in colonial times
C but beware of
D for some time now
E for the most part
F given the widespread disapproval
G however
H in fact
I in spite of
J which could motivate people
K of the least concern
L on the other hand
M while the antelope-like springbok
N walking in the bush

_____

_____ (1) is the symbol of the national rugby team, the elegant blue crane is the country's national bird. South African wildlife boasts some unique and amazing creatures, from the world's smallest mammal, the tiny pygmy shrew, to the great white shark. You can swim with penguins, _____ (2) the tall ostrich, which cannot swim or fly but has a powerful kick. _____ (3), you could meet cheeky baboons, but also the Cape Cobra, one of the deadliest snakes in the world.

_____ (4), South Africa's most famous wildlife is probably the Big Five: lions, leopards, rhinoceros, elephants and Cape buffalo. _____ (5) being very dangerous, these animals aren't invincible. They have all been classed as vulnerable by the International Union for the Conservation of Nature. In terms of conservation, the Cape buffalo is _____ (6) as the species remains widespread, with a global population estimated at nearly 900,000 animals, though this has made it the most popular animal to hunt.

_____ (7) the biggest game hunting destination in the world, this practice has undergone significant changes in implementation and public perception over the last century. _____ (8), big game hunting had connotations of aristocracy and glamour. Today, game hunting still belongs to the elite and privileged, thanks to the hefty price tags, but _____ (9), associations of prestige and sportsmanship have been stripped away.

_____ (10) and population perils, game hunters have shifted the way they present the practice. _____ (11), supporters have been trying to persuade the public that hunting is helping to protect, rather than destroy, the animals as it can aid conservation efforts by generating revenue necessary to protect the animals and their habitat. Hunters also claim that they are helping to control animal populations and support local communities by providing jobs and income, _____ (12) to protect animals from poaching.
Critics, _____ (13), argue that up to now, only minimal profits have reached local communities, and that for hunting to support conservation, appropriate management of funds raised, and sustainable allocation of animal quotas are indispensable. _____ (14), reality has shown that inadequate monitoring makes these factors difficult to control. Game hunting might help conservation when managed appropriately, but there are ways to help the Big Five that are much more appealing to animal lovers.

b Explain the meaning of the following words and phrases from the text on page 41.

1 widespread _____
2 game _____
3 hefty _____
4 price tags _____
5 stripped away _____
6 revenue _____
7 poaching _____
8 quotas _____

15 Conservation. Read this encyclopedia entry about the International Union for Conservation of Nature (IUCN) and complete it with the present perfect or present perfect progressive form of the verbs in the box.

> assess ■ become ■ be criticized ■ incorporate ■ be involved ■ play ■ search ■ spark ■ widen ■ work

The IUCN, which was founded in 1948, is an international organization which _____ (1) hard in the field of conservation. Over the decades, it _____ (2) its focus beyond conservation and it _____ (3) projects related to sustainability. The organization, which _____ (4) best known to the public for its Red List of threatened species, _____ (5) the conservation status of species worldwide since 1964.

The IUCN _____ (6) an important role in setting up organizations such as the World Conservation Centre. Since 2005, it _____ _____ (7) in minimum energy consumption and zero-carbon construction projects by integrating energy-saving materials. Since the emergence of the concept of nature-based solutions in environmental sciences and nature conservation contexts, the IUCN _____ (8) for solutions to work with ecosystems rather than relying on conventional engineering interventions to adapt to climate change effects, while protecting natural ecosystems and biodiversity. However, the IUCN _____ (9) for placing the interests of nature over those of indigenous peoples and its closer relations with the business sector _____ (10) heated debates.

Workshop 2

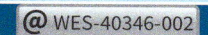

→ students' book, pages 64/65

@ WES-40346-002

16 Poaching

a Listen to this interview by Sam from *Four Corners* with Dr Maya Jensen, a rhino conservationist in which she provided insights into her efforts and initiatives. Then complete these sentences about the first part of the interview using the information in brackets.

1 When Sam asked Dr Jensen about how she got into rhino conservation, she explained _____. (*passion, begin, child*)

2 She described how _____. (*be captivated*)

3 When Sam wanted to know about the challenges, Dr Jensen said _____. (*face many, most critical poaching*)

4 She went on to explain _____. (*people think, magic potion*)

5 She added _____. (*habitat loss, threaten survival*)

b Listen again and do the tasks.

1 List two initiatives that Dr Jensen is talking about.

_____

2 Outline the operation that Dr Jensen sees as one success story.

_____

3 Summarize the message that Dr Jensen wants to share with the world.

_____

forty-three **43**

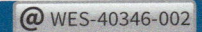

Practice: Making a difference

17 Voluntourism. After her holiday, Tricia looks into volunteer tourism in South Africa. Read the comments she found online. With a partner, agree if they are positive or negative.
- Volunteer tourism does not necessarily have positive impacts.
- Voluntourism projects are often misrepresented.
- People and Places has won a Responsible Tourism award.
- At least 80% of the profits are returned to the community.
- The most expensive trips are likely to be the least responsible.

18 A debate about voluntourism

a Listen to part of a radio interview debate about voluntourism and do the tasks.

1 Explain who Dr Hayley Mills is and outline her position regarding voluntourism.

2 Say who Andrea Haas is and what she thinks about voluntourism.

3 Tick (✓) the ideas that are <u>not</u> mentioned in the debate.
- [ ] a The environmental impact of voluntourism.
- [ ] b Short-term nature and lack of proper management lead to limited impact and potential harm.
- [ ] c The impact of voluntourism projects is limited and not sustainable in some cases.
- [ ] d The potential for loss of local control.
- [ ] e The practice of voluntourism may lead to cultural appropriation.
- [ ] f The need for proper screening, training and support of volunteers to ensure a positive and sustainable impact.
- [ ] g Positive impact on communities through volunteer work and cultural exchange.
- [ ] h Voluntourism may contribute to over-tourism and overcrowding in some places.
- [ ] i The cost of voluntourism can be a hurdle for many people who want to participate.

b Listen again and do the tasks.

1 Explain why Andrea Haas thinks that volunteer tourism does not actually address the root cause of the problem.
2 Outline Dr Mills' response to Andrea Haas' argument.
3 Summarize how Dr Mills' agency ensures that volunteers are able to make a positive impact in the communities they serve.
4 Say what Andrea Haas' final point about volunteer tourism is.

19 For or against? Read this summary of the debate on voluntourism. Complete the gaps with the present perfect or present perfect progressive form of the verbs in the box.

> advocate ■ attract (2x) ■ become ■ benefit ■ criticize ■ emerge ■ evolve ■
> gain ■ point out ■ provide ■ undermine

Over the years, voluntourism _____ (1) both praise and criticism due to its complex nature and impact on local communities. While the concept of voluntourism _____ (2) in popularity in recent years, there are those who support it and those who are against it.

Supporters of voluntourism believe that the practice provides a great opportunity for travellers to make a really positive impact on local communities. Therefore, they _____ continuously _____ (3) for voluntourism as an instrument of cross-cultural understanding and cultural exchange.

As a consequence, voluntourism _____ (4) more popular and _____ (5) a more responsible and socially-conscious traveller. And it is true that communities in certain areas _____ (6) from the hands-on assistance voluntourists _____ (7). Opponents of voluntourism, on the other hand, _____ consistently _____ (8) the practice for being more about fulfilling the personal interests and egos of the volunteers rather than actually helping the communities. Critics _____ (9) instances where voluntourism initiatives _____ (10) local professionals' efforts. As the debate _____, (11) more research _____ (12) highlighting the need for well-structured voluntourism programmes.

20 WRITING FOCUS: Writing a magazine advert

a Work with a partner to write a magazine advert for a volunteering holiday in South Africa. First, decide on the details of your advert. Make notes.
- Will the programme take place in a city or in the wild?
- Will volunteers be helping people, animals or the environment?

b You should both offer reasons, negotiate a choice and then agree on your volunteering holiday. Do your research. Decide what you need to know and divide the tasks between you.

c Write your advert, thinking about your target audience and how you can make your advert look attractive. Use evocative language so your programme will appeal to others, but don't forget to give factual information and tips.

d Share your advert with two or three other pairs. Then vote on the most appealing advert.

Music matters

21 **The development of music in South Africa.** Read the conversation between Alex and Jake about South African music and answer the questions.

A Hey, Jake! Have you ever thought about the evolution of South African music? It's pretty fascinating how it's changed over the years.

J Totally, man! It's like a blend of so many different cultures and influences. I mean, you've got traditional African rhythms, colonial European stuff, and even modern hip-hop and pop vibes now.

A Right! And it's so cool how they've managed to preserve those traditional elements while still creating something unique and new. Have you heard of Maskandi music? It's this Zulu genre that's all about storytelling and guitar playing.

J Yeah, I've heard a bit about it. They're passing down their history through the music, right? And then you've got Isicathamiya, which is like a vocal harmony style that started in the mines during the apartheid era. It's all about community and unity.

A Definitely. And remember that time we saw a video about Kwaito music? It's like hip-hop, but with its own twist. It was a form of resistance against apartheid.

J Oh yeah, that was eye-opening! The beats were so infectious, and the lyrics had this raw honesty to them. Music was used to communicate political messages and bring people together during the tough times.

A And speaking of tough times, jazz played a huge role, too. Miriam Makeba and Hugh Masekela used their music to protest against apartheid on the international stage.

J Right on. They brought global attention to what was happening in South Africa. And let's not forget Brenda Fassie, the 'Queen of African Pop'. She was like a cultural icon and her music was a blend of pop, disco and traditional sounds.

A Oh, for sure! And now there's this whole new wave of South African artists who are blending genres even more. Sho Madjozi, for example, fuses rap with traditional Tsonga vibes, creating this super catchy and unique sound.

J Yeah, she's definitely pushing boundaries. And what about Amapiano? It's the genre that's blowing up not only in South Africa but internationally. It's like a mix of house, jazz and kwaito, and it's got everyone dancing.

A It's crazy how music keeps evolving, man.

J And it's awesome that we're witnessing the next chapter being written by our own generation. Who knows what kind of sounds we'll be hearing in the years to come!

Brenda Fassie and Nelson Mandela, 1993

1 What influences have contributed to the development of South African music?

2 What is Maskandi music, and what is its significance in South African culture?

3 How does Isicathamiya music reflect the historical context in which it originated?

4 How did Kwaito music serve as a form of resistance during the apartheid era?

5 What was unique about Brenda Fassie's music and her impact on South African culture?
_____

6 How would you describe the musical style of Sho Madjozi, and what makes her stand out?
_____

22 From the 1950s

a Now listen to a podcast about a more in-depth look at the South African music scene since the 1950s. Identify the following words in the podcast and match them to their meanings.

1 touchstone   a what happens after and often because of something else
2 in the wake of   b containing important new ideas and influencing later work
3 slip back   c become firmly established or widely accepted
4 seminal   d an established standard by which something is judged
5 crossover   e the process of changing from one activity or style to another
6 take hold   f go somewhere quickly so you are not noticed

b Listen again and do the tasks.

1 Explain what Sophiatown was and what it represented in South Africa.
_____
_____

2 Describe who Miriam Makeba was including her role in the African jazz scene.
_____
_____

3 Outline what led to the end of the musically vital era of Sophiatown.
_____
_____

DJs Candii & Lula Odiba at YFM radio station which specializes in playing urban music such as Kwaito, Hip Hop and R&B

4 Explain who Abdullah Ibrahim was, including his contribution to South African music.
_____
_____

5 Say what the 'Alternative Afrikaans' movement was and why it emerged.
_____
_____

6 Explain what Fokofpolisiekar is and what it has done for Afrikaans music.
_____
_____

c Pick one of the styles or people from **21** or **22** that interests you and do some research. Write a text (150 words) with some background information explaining why you find them interesting.

Practice: South African style

23 Sensible fashion. Complete what a young South African says about fashion with the modal verbs (*not*) *need to, should, have to, might, can't, must*. You can use them more than once.

How important is fashion to me? Well, I believe that fashion is a way of expressing myself and my individuality. Although I _____ (1) (*follow*) every trend or purchase every popular item.
I _____ (2) (*experiment*) with different styles, but ultimately,
I _____ (3) (*wear*) what makes me happy. I love mixing different pieces to create my own unique style. I _____ (4) (*wear*) something colourful one day and then a more chic look the next, but I _____ (5) (*feel*) like myself. I _____ (6) (*let*) clothes change my personality.
Everyone _____ (7) (*dress*) in a way that really makes them feel comfortable. We _____ (8) (*follow*) any specific rules just because a designer says so! Of course, we _____ (9) (*dress*) appropriately.
But otherwise, we _____ (10) (*be*) free to wear what we want.
My mother always says I _____ (11) (*invest*) in quality pieces that will last me a long time, and she's right. I _____ (12) (*say*), I really enjoy trying out new styles as I grow up.
There is also another aspect of fashion that we _____ (13) (*bear*) in mind: sustainability. We _____ (14) (*consider*) the environmental impact of the fashion industry and try to choose sustainable and ethical clothing options. We _____ (15) (*remember*) that fashion is not just about looking good but also making conscious choices for ourselves and the planet.

24 Haute Afrika

a A young South African designer has become a success story in the fashion world. Read the introduction to a short film about her. Why do you think she called her brand *Haute Afrika*?

> Gracia Bampile knew at the age of only seven that she wanted to be in the fashion industry and now, years later, she owns a clothing brand that takes pride in African couture, 'Haute Afrika'. With no formal fashion training background, she has become a trendsetter in the booming fashion industry. She has dressed African TV personalities, actors, presenters, singers and rappers. She tells her interviewer how she works.

b Watch the video about *Haute Afrika* and do the tasks.

1. Describe the *Haute Afrika* factory and the impression it made on you.
   _____

2. Explain why Gracia's mother stopped buying her clothes.
   _____

3. Outline the significance of the African print bow ties to Gracia.
   _____

4. Summarize what influencer Mihlali Ndamase says about Gracia's print clothing.
   _____

5. Point out how Chinese mass-produced copies of *Haute Afrika* clothing affect Gracia.
   _____

c Match the sentence parts to make a list of top tips for successful fashion design.

1. In order to succeed,
2. Your designs don't have to
3. In other words, you mustn't
4. To increase sales, you ought to
5. For popular designs, you may be obliged to

a. accept cheap mass-produced copies.
b. feel afraid of being different.
c. you have to be creative.
d. make use of social media platforms.
e. be the same as everyone else's.

25 Youth trends

a Read the article and complete it with the words and phrases in the box.

> as for ■ as with ■ due to ■ from ■ however ■ in addition ■ in conclusion ■ it's all about ■ such as ■ to

_____ (1) most countries, youth fashion trends in South Africa are influenced by global fashion and cultural movements. _____ (2), there are also unique local factors that shape South African youth fashion. One major trend that has emerged in recent years is a
5 celebration of African heritage. This is reflected in the popularity of prints and fabrics that are traditionally associated with African cultures, _____ (3) shweshwe, kente and Ankara. These prints are often incorporated into contemporary designs, creating a fusion of old and new.
10 Another trend that has taken hold is a preference for comfortable and practical clothing. This is perhaps _____ (4) the warm climate and an emphasis on outdoor activities. South African youth are also known for their love of streetwear.

continued on page 50

_____ (5) oversized T-shirts _____ (6) statement sneakers, streetwear has become a staple in many young South Africans' wardrobes. Social media has played a significant role in popularizing streetwear, with influencers and celebrities often showcasing their latest cutting-edge looks on social media. In terms of colour, bright hues are popular, as well as earthy tones that reflect the country's natural beauty. _____ (7) accessories, chunky necklaces and hoop earrings are all the rage.

_____ (8), South Africa's youth of today are more accepting of non-binary identities than their predecessors, and their clothing reflects this. The unisex appeal of streetwear is represented in high fashion as women wear trouser suits and ties and **sport crew cuts**. Men have taken longer to become gender-neutral, but they're **making inroads**, with many opting for longer hair, candy-coloured clothing, nail polish and eyeliner. _____ (9) living, loving and working in a **gender non-conforming way**. **Leading the pack** are celebrity rapper Mx Blouse and artistic duo FAKA. _____ (10), youth fashion trends in South Africa are a mix of global influences and unique local factors.

b Look back at the text and find words that match the definitions.

1. the external form or outline of something   _____
2. a basic or an essential item that is always in demand and regularly used   _____
3. exhibiting something in a way that highlights its features or qualities   _____
4. innovative, advanced or at the forefront of a particular field or industry   _____

c Explain the meanings of these **bold** expressions from the article.

1. to sport a crew cut _____
2. making inroads _____
3. gender non-conforming way _____
4. leading the pack _____

26 SPEAKING FOCUS: No jeans, please !

a Listen to Ben, an American schoolboy, describe what the dress code and fashions are at his school. Discuss the similarities or differences with your school with a partner.

b Now listen to Kylie who has to wear a uniform at her school in South Africa. Talk to your partner and make comparisons with Ben's situation.

c Discuss the reasons for and against school uniforms. Then record a podcast, summarizing both sides of the argument before giving your own opinion on uniforms at school.

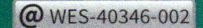

Analysing song lyrics

27 *Stimela (The Coal Train)*

a Read the introduction to the song *Stimela* (*The Coal Train*). Can you predict what the song is going to be about? Watch the video and check your ideas.

> Hugh Masekela (1939 – 2018), legendary trumpet player and singer/songwriter, wrote 'Stimela' while still in exile following the political unrest surrounding the 1960 Sharpeville Massacre. One of the great anthems in the struggle against apartheid, 'Stimela' was first released in 1974 on the album 'I am Not Afraid'.

b Watch the video again and read the lyrics. Make a list of the words you don't know and share your list with a partner. Find the meaning of the words.

Stimela (The Coal Train)
There is a train that comes from Namibia and Malawi
There is a train that comes from Zambia and Zimbabwe
5 There is a train that comes from Angola and Mozambique
From Lesotho, from Botswana, from Swaziland
From all the hinterlands of Southern and Central Africa
10 This train carries young and old, African men
Who are conscripted to come and work on contract
In the gold and mineral mines of Johannesburg
And its surrounding metropolis, sixteen hours
15 or more a day
For almost no pay
Deep, deep, deep down in the belly of the earth
When they are digging and drilling that shiny mighty evasive stone
20 Or when they dish that mish mesh mush food
Into their iron plates with the iron shank
Or when they sit in their stinking, funky, filthy
Flea-ridden barracks and hostels
They think about the loved ones they may
25 never see again
Because they might already have been forcibly removed
From where they last left them
Or wantonly murdered in the dead of night
30 By roving, marauding gangs of no particular origin
We are told
They think about their lands, and their herds
That were taken away from them
35 With the gun, and the bomb, and the teargas, the gatling and the cannon
And when they hear that Choo-Choo train
A-chugging, and a pumping, and a smoking, and a pushing
40 A pumping, a crying and a steaming and a-chugging and
A whooo whooo!
They always cuss, and they curse the coal train
The coal train that brought them to Johannesburg
45 Whooo whooo! [...]

Coal Train, Masekela, Hugh. We've got rhythm music/Rondor Musikverlag GmbH, Berlin

28 **Your analysis.** Make notes on the lyrics of *Stimela*. Find examples of literary devices such as repetition and alliteration. List interesting words or phrases. Use your notes to do the tasks.
1 Describe the main theme of *Stimela* in your own words.
2 Give examples of repetition and explain the point Masekela makes when he uses it.
3 Note down where alliteration is used in the song.
4 Say where the song contrasts a child's language with the harsh reality of the situation.
5 Find and comment on the lines which describe the brutality faced by families left behind.

Mediation

29 **The energy crisis in South Africa.** You are participating in a European youth conference about the energy crisis and climate change. The discussion is about the situation in different countries worldwide. You remember having read this article in a German magazine. Write a short text (150 words) in English describing the problems and challenges the inhabitants of Capetown face daily. You should also mention the likely causes and the consequences.

> **Wie auf der Titanic, nur zappenduster: Wenn der Stromausfall zum Alltag gehört**
> Von Bartholomäus Grill
>
> Südafrika gilt vielen als das wirtschaftliche Vorzeigeland Afrikas. Doch inzwischen fällt der Strom hier fast jeden Tag aus, oft für viele Stunden. Ein Erlebnisbericht über die alltäglichen Folgen.
> Schon wieder kein frisch aufgebrühter Kaffee zum Start in den Tag. Aus dem
> 5 Durchlauferhitzer kommt nur lauwarmes Wasser. [...]
> **Good morning, Cape Town!**
> Ich fahre in mein Büro in die Innenstadt, dort sollte es Strom geben. Der Verkehr staut sich, die Ampeln sind ausgefallen. Das Café gegenüber vom Bürogebäude hat leider auch keinen Cappuccino. "Blackout", sagt der Barista. Ich steige die fünf Etagen zu
> 10 meinem Office hoch, das Risiko, im Fahrstuhl stecken zu bleiben, ist zu hoch. [...]
> Mittags das gleiche Problem: Im Restaurant gleich nebenan bleibt die Küche kalt. [...] Im Supermarkt wird es plötzlich zappenduster, die Kundinnen und Kunden irren in den Gängen herum. Der Dieselgenerator springt mit Verzögerung an. Die Kühlregale für Fisch und Meeresfrüchte sind gähnend leer, auf einem handgeschriebenen Zettel steht die
> 15 Entschuldigung der Filialleiterin: "Sorry, Kühlkette wegen load shedding unterbrochen".
> **330 Millionen Euro am Tag gehen verloren**
> Load shedding. [...] Es bedeutet "Lastabwurf" und ist die euphemistische Umschreibung eines Notstands, der Südafrika seit Jahren heimsucht [...]: Der Strom wird mehrmals täglich stundenlang abgestellt, um den landesweiten Zusammenbruch des
> 20 Elektrizitätsnetzes zu vermeiden.
> Das Debakel hat einen Namen: Eskom, der nationale Energieversorger. Dieser Konzern ist der wichtigste Geldesel der Regierungspartei African National Congress (ANC), [...]. Eskom wurde zum Synonym für Missmanagement, Planlosigkeit, Inkompetenz und Korruption.
> 25 Die Kohlekraftwerke sind alt, überlastet und werden schlecht gewartet. Wenn ein neues Führungsteam versucht, die Missstände zu beheben, kommt es zu Sabotageakten [...]. André de Ruyter, der Chef von Eskom, schmiss vor Kurzem hin; er hatte einen Giftanschlag überlebt, in seinem Kaffee war Zyanid.
> Die ökonomischen Kollateralschäden der Stromausfälle sind enorm. Experten schätzen,
> 30 dass der ohnehin angeschlagenen Volkwirtschaft Südafrikas bis zu sechs Milliarden Rand pro Tag verloren gehen, umgerechnet rund 330 Millionen Euro. Das schädigt das Image der Kaprepublik, schreckt Investoren ab und beschleunigt die Talfahrt der Landeswährung. [...]
> **Privathaushalte rüsten mit Generatoren auf**
> 35 [...] ich habe mittlerweile gelernt, mit den Kalamitäten irgendwie zurechtzukommen und meinen Tagesablauf entsprechend angepasst. Es gibt schließlich eine App von Eskom, die die wechselnden Zeiten und Stufen der Stromausfälle ankündigt.

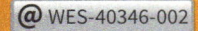

Trotzdem platzt mir manchmal der Kragen, denn die Informationen sind oft falsch und irreführend. Dann warte ich vergeblich an der Tankstelle, weil die Benzinpumpen nicht
40 funktionieren. [...]
Und so folgt ein Malheur auf das andere. Beim Bäcker gibt es kein Brot, weil er nicht backen kann. Die Metzgerei hat mangels Kühlenergie stundenweise geschlossen. Zuhause steht die Waschmaschine still. Der Kühlschrank gibt wegen der ständigen Abschaltungen den Geist auf. [...]
45 Viele Geschäfte und Privathaushalte rüsten mit Dieselgeneratoren auf. Auch wir überlegen, uns einen zuzulegen, um die stromlosen Phasen zu überbrücken, aber die Geräte haben sich extrem verteuert und sind gerade ausverkauft. [...]
Was ist der Unterschied zwischen der Titanic und Südafrika?
Besonders unheimlich wird es bei nächtlichen Blackouts. Dann gehen die Lichter in
50 allen Häusern aus, die Straßenbeleuchtung erlischt und Oranjezicht, unser schönes Stadtviertel, versinkt in Finsternis. Wir verbringen den Abend im Kerzenschein und gehen früh ins Bett. [...]
In solchen Momenten fällt mir ein Witz ein, den sich die Kapstädter in diesen Krisentagen gerne erzählen.
55 Frage: Was ist der Unterschied zwischen der Titanic und Südafrika?
Antwort: Die Titanic war hell erleuchtet, als sie unterging.

Source (abbreviated): Bartholomäus Grill, „Wie auf der Titanic, nur zappenduster: Wenn der Stromausfall zum Alltag gehört", Stern, 29.01.2013, https://www.stern.de/gesellschaft/ erfahrungsbericht-suedafrika--unser-leben-ohne-strom-in-kapstadt-33142272.html [29.08.2023]

30 **Comparison of electricity generation in Africa in 2021.** You have done further research into energy generation in Africa and have come across these statistics. Write a report (100 words) in German, comparing two of the major energy producing countries in Africa (diagrams 1 and 2). Put these figures into perspective considering all of Africa as shown in diagram 3.

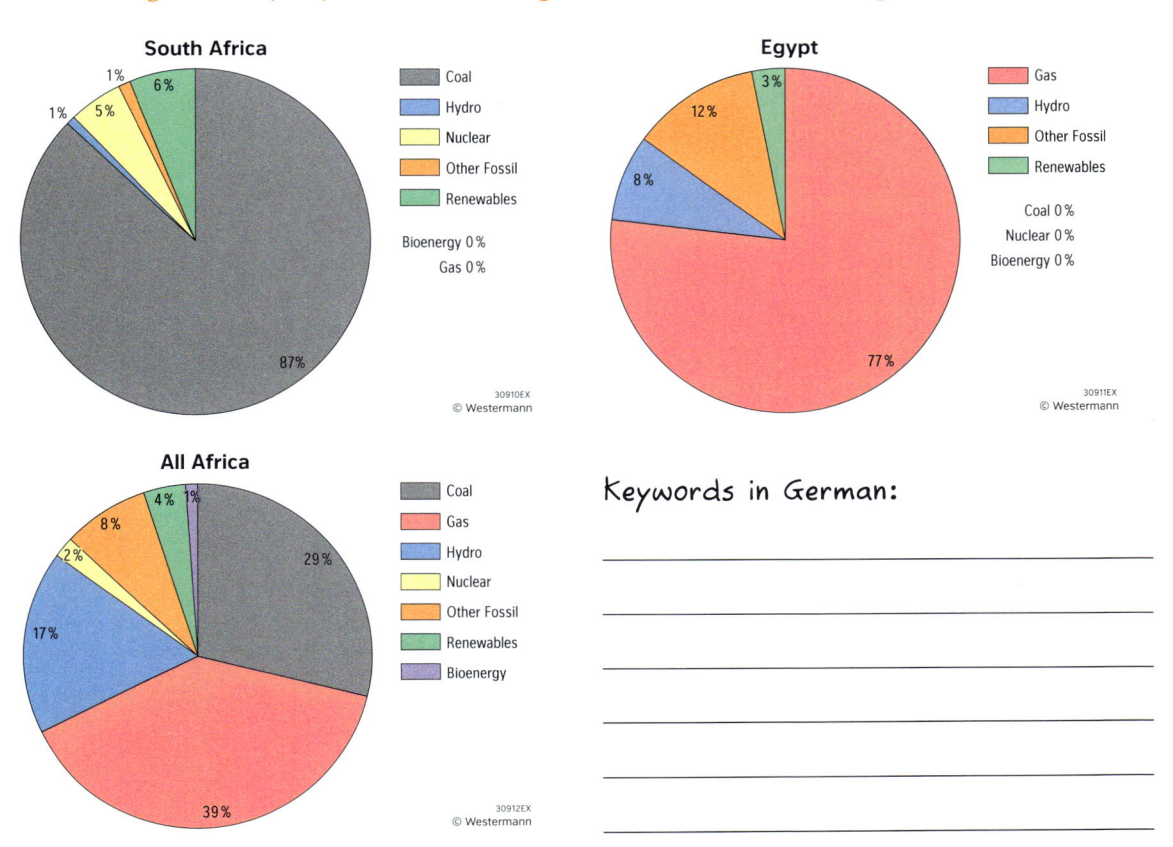

South Africa
- Coal: 87%
- Hydro: 1%
- Nuclear: 5%
- Other Fossil: 1%
- Renewables: 6%
- Bioenergy: 0%
- Gas: 0%

Egypt
- Gas: 77%
- Hydro: 8%
- Other Fossil: 12%
- Renewables: 3%
- Coal: 0%
- Nuclear: 0%
- Bioenergy: 0%

All Africa
- Coal: 29%
- Gas: 39%
- Hydro: 17%
- Nuclear: 2%
- Other Fossil: 8%
- Renewables: 4%
- Bioenergy: 1%

Keywords in German:
_____
_____
_____
_____
_____
_____

My review

1 About India and Pakistan

a
1 whose death at the hands of the police in 1977 shocked the world
2 which he founded in 1969
3 who heard about Biko's death on the BBC news
4 which was released in 1997
5 which is in the song
6 which was held in honour of Nelson Mandela's seventieth birthday
7 which included phrases in isiXhosa

b
Possible anwers:
1 *Cry Freedom*, which is set in South Africa, is about Steve Biko's final days.
2 The film, which stars Denzel Washington and Kevin Kline, was shot in Zimbabwe rather than South Africa.
3 Donald Wood, who was an South African journalist, became close friends with Biko.
4 Richard Attenborough, who directed films like *Ghandi* and *A Bridge Too Far*, directed *Cry Freedom*.
5 A list which contains the names of many people who died in police custody appears at the end of the film.
6 *Cry Freedom*, which won many awards, was nominated for three Oscars.

2 About sports and politics
1 had not supported
2 would not be
3 would probably have turned out
4 had not pushed
5 had told
6 would have thought
7 work
8 is / will be
9 had not recognized
10 would not have reacted
11 had not seen
12 would not have felt
13 work
14 can achieve
15 am
16 will put

3 About animal and conservation
1 have you been interested
2 have always been drawn to
3 Do you ever worry
4 have been spending
5 have heard
6 have been diving
7 have only been attacked
8 have lost
9 has been increasing
10 have even seen
11 have been complaining
12 have done
13 have never felt
14 has been

4 About diversity

a
1 segregated
2 racial
3 inclusivity
4 coloured
5 sexuality
6 inequality
7 able-bodied

b
1 must
2 ought to / should
3 shouldn't
4 need to
5 must have been
6 might have been
7 must
8 should
9 'll have to
10 must

Living together

1 **Defining a nation.** Scottish student Ellie is spending a year at a Cape Breton Island high school. Read the beginning of a report for her classmates at home and answer the questions.

> Defining a nation with six time zones is not easy. What could an English speaker in Vancouver possibly have in common with a Francophone 5,000 km away in Quebec City? What could either have in common with a Gaelic speaker here in
> 5 Nova Scotia? There are also over 200 ethnic groups across the land to consider.
> Today, nearly one fifth of Canadians are able to converse in both English and French, and immigration has added over 215 other languages to the mix, the most important of which is
> 10 Mandarin. Immigration is currently high, with newcomers accounting for two-thirds of the country's recent population growth. Diversity is a core element of the country's identity and a word Canadians use when describing themselves.

1 Why is defining a nation with six time zones considered difficult?

2 What does Ellie suggest is at the heart of the country's identity?

2 **First Nations people**

a Ellie has looked for information to better understand who the First Nations are and how to correctly refer to them. Read the text and do the tasks.

> Canada's First Nations are Indigenous peoples who are recognized as distinct from Métis or Inuit. According to the Constitution Act of 1982, Aboriginal peoples in Canada include Indian (First Nations), Inuit and Métis peoples. In Canada, First Nations people are also known as Indians, Natives or Amerindians, but these names may have negative
> 5 connotations. The term 'Indian' has specific legal contexts. The Indian Act is the document that governs the federal government's relationship with First Nations people. This act maintains an Indian Register, which is an official record of all First Nations people recognized as Status Indians.
> Historically, 'Indian' was the common term for First Nations heritage in Canada, until
> 10 'First Nations' was coined in the 1980s with the Declaration of the First Nations by chiefs in Ottawa. The National Indian Brotherhood, now the Assembly of First Nations, was renamed in 1982. 'First Nations' symbolically acknowledges them as foundational to Canada's origin, emphasizing their sovereignty and pursuit of self-determination. Nonetheless, this term isn't used by Indigenous peoples outside Canada.
> 15 While 'First Nations' is a broad label, community members often identify with specific groups. For instance, a Kanyen'kehà:ka (Mohawk) individual from Akwesasne, belonging to the Bear clan, might use more accurate identifiers than 'First Nations' or 'Indigenous'.

1 Research and explain what the origin of the term Métis is.

2 Outline the key points of the article.

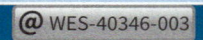

b Ellie has read about people who have made their home in Canada. Complete the sentences from Ravi's story with the correct past tense of the verbs in brackets.

1 One evening while my partner Ashley and I _____ (*have*) dinner here in Toronto, we got talking to a couple who _____ (*ask*) how long I _____ (*live*) in Canada and what _____ (*prompt*) me to come here.

2 My decision to move to Canada _____ (*begin*) in the US where I _____ (*never feel*) completely accepted, no doubt partly due to my status as a 'non-resident alien'.

3 I _____ (*grow up*) with my three siblings in India before I _____ (*emigrate*) to the USA in the hope of a better life. But after many years, I _____ (*still live*) there on a visa. One day in early February, I _____ (*decide*) 'enough is enough'. I _____ (*hear*) so many positive reports about Canada, so I _____ (*start*) the application process.

4 Unfortunately, everything was delayed due to the COVID-19 pandemic, a hurdle I _____ (*not anticipate*), but finally one morning while I _____ (*get*) ready to meet a friend for lunch, a letter _____ (*arrive*).

5 Overnight I _____ (*go*) from living in the US, a country where I _____ (*find*) new friends but where the authorities _____ (*refuse*) to accept me, to Canada, a country that _____ (*offer*) me hope in the form of a permanent residency card.

6 The highlight at the end of that year _____ (*be*) when I _____ (*return*) to Canada after visiting friends in the US. As you can imagine, I _____ (*feel*) rather nervous at immigration. 'Welcome home,' _____ (*say*) the officer – two words I _____ (*never hear*) during my time in the States.

3 Migrate to Canada!

a Listen to a *Four Corners* podcast about Canada and do the tasks.

1. Explain why people prefer to migrate to Canada than to the US.
   _____
   _____
   _____

2. Outline Canada's attitude to multiculturalism.
   _____
   _____

3. Outline why Canada is considered one of the most inclusive countries in the world.
   _____
   _____

4. Describe Canada's education system.
   _____
   _____

5. Summarize the Canadian healthcare system.
   _____
   _____

6. List the benefits enjoyed by workers.
   _____
   _____

7. Say why Canada is one of the safest countries in the world.
   _____
   _____

b Listen again and explain the meaning of the phrases.

1. melting pot _____
   _____

2. mosaic culture _____
   _____

3. stepping into the spotlight _____

Practice: Being yourself

4 **Native history.** Read the text about how Thomas King wrote his book *The Inconvenient Indian* and complete it with the verbs in brackets in the correct tense.

When Thomas King _____ (1) (*think*) about how to write *The Inconvenient Indian*, initially he _____ (2) (*not know*) how to make a non-fiction topic readable. Although he _____ (3) (*read*) some very good books about native history, he _____ (4) (*not be*) sure how many people actually _____ (5) (*enjoy*) reading such works. Therefore, he _____ (6) (*challenge*) himself to take the field of non-fiction and merge it with what he _____ (7) (*learn*) as a literary writer.

He _____ (8) (*try*) to use some of the many skills that he _____ (9) (*acquire*) in creating character and dialogue in this non-fiction piece. While he _____ (10) (*consider*) how best to approach this topic, he _____ (11) (*realize*) that one of the problems with native history is that much of it is gruesome. He knew that if he _____ (12) (*just repeat*) the historical facts or _____ (13) (*just revisit*) those moments, he could lose his reader pretty quickly. He _____ (14) (*need*) give-and-take between historical fact and readability. After he _____ (15) (*work*) on the book for quite a while, he _____ (16) (*discover*) that using the first person _____ (17) (*definitely not work*). He _____ (18) (*feel*) that dialogue would make the writing easier and provide him with a second voice that could ask questions.

Workshop 3

→ students' book, pages 96/97

5 Literature class

a Emma and Aki are in Ellie's class. Listen to their conversation and do the tasks.

1 Say who they are talking about.
___

2 Say what book Emma is reading.
___

3 Outline which other books are mentioned.
___

4 Summarize what recommendation Emma makes and why.
___
___
___

b Aki has read *Girl, Woman, Other* and has recorded a presentation for the class. Listen to her presentation and do the tasks.

1 Describe what *Girl, Woman, Other* is about.
___
___

2 Outline who the protagonists are.
___
___

3 Explain the significance of chapter four in *Girl, Woman, Other*.
___
___

4 Outline one thing that Aki particularly likes about the novel.
___
___

6 Your choice. Write about which of the novels from this section you would like to read, and which you would not. Give reasons.
___
___
___
___
___

7 SPEAKING FOCUS: *Part-time Woman*

a Talk to a partner about the photo of Vivek Shraya, a Canadian musician, writer and visual artist. Describe the singer and discuss your reaction to the photo. Speculate on Shraya as a musician.

b Watch part of an interview with Vivek Shraya and do the tasks.

1 Summarize how the interviewer introduces Vivek Shraya and why their book has attracted attention.

_____
_____

2 Outline how Vivek Shraya describes themselves.

_____
_____

3 Say what they learned when they were in their 20s.

_____
_____

4 Say what happened when they were in their 30s.

_____
_____

5 Explain what pressure they suffered and how they eventually resolved the situation.

_____
_____

c Vivek Shraya recorded a song called *Part-time Woman*. Discuss with your partner what you think it is about.

d Listen to the song. Discuss your reactions to the lyrics.

e Find an artist, a performer or a writer in Germany similar to Vivek Shraya. Do some research and write an article about them (150 words).

_____
_____
_____
_____
_____
_____

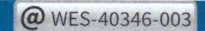

Rethinking climate change

8 **Environmental literacy**

a Brainstorm the environmental issues you think Canada has to tackle. To help you to discuss them, check your understanding of the words in the wordle. Choose four or five words that seem important and make a note of your reasons.

b Compare your words with a partner from another group.

9 **A changing climate.** Aki is writing an essay on climate change. Complete the first part with the verbs in brackets in the correct future tense – the *will* future or future perfect.

Climate change has become a growing concern for our planet, and its consequences _____ (1) (*be*) more severe if we don't take action now. By the year 2050, climate change _____ (2) (*dramatically alter*) the planet as we know it today.

Scientists predict that by 2050 the average global temperature _____ (3) (*increase*) by 2 degrees Celsius, which _____ (4) (*cause*) significant changes in weather patterns. We _____ (5) (*experience*) an increase in extreme weather conditions, including more frequent and severe hurricanes, tornadoes and floods. The oceans _____ (6) (*rise*) by several feet, causing floods and erosion and displacing millions of people living in coastal areas. Entire cities _____ (7) (*completely disappear*) under water, and many _____ (8) (*be*) uninhabitable due to the rising sea levels. It is also expected that many plant and animal species _____ (9) (*become*) extinct due to the changing climate. Many species _____ (10) (*not be able to*) adapt to the rapidly changing environment, leading to their demise. The impact of these extinctions _____ (11) (*affect*) the survival of other species, including humans.

In addition to the physical impact of climate change, there _____ (12) (*be*) significant economic and social consequences. As droughts become more and more frequent, we _____ (13) (*see*) a decline in agricultural productivity, which _____ (14) (*lead*) to food shortages and higher prices. The increased frequency of extreme weather events _____ (15) (*also result*) in higher insurance costs and damage to property, which _____ (16) (*put*) a strain on many families and communities.

Workshop 3

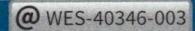

→ students' book, pages 98/99

10 **Climate change in the Great Lakes.** Watch the video and do the tasks.

1. Say what the Great Lakes basin is and describe its importance.
2. List some of the impacts of climate change on the Great Lakes.
3. Say why climate change is considered to be a threat multiplier.
4. Explain the impact of declining lake ice.
5. Explain how changing water levels are affecting the Great Lakes.
6. Outline why coastal wetlands are particularly vulnerable to changing climate conditions and water levels.
7. Explain what is being done to address the impacts of climate change on the Great Lakes.

11 *An Inconvenient Sequel: Truth to Power*

a Former US Vice President Al Gore was awarded a Nobel Prize in 2007. Find out why, and research what his book and documentary were about.

b More than a decade after *An Inconvenient Truth*, carbon emissions were still causing concern. Talk about what the data shows and what you know about the situation today.

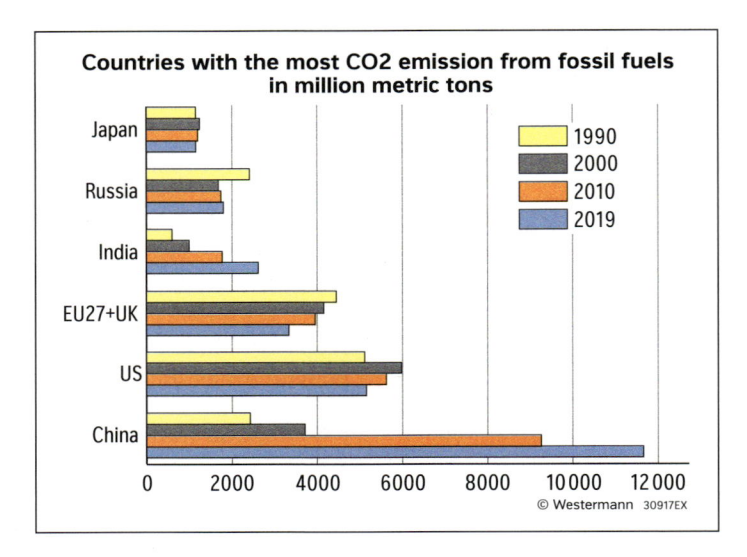

Countries with the most CO_2 emission from fossil fuels in million metric tons (Japan, Russia, India, EU27+UK, US, China — years 1990, 2000, 2010, 2019)

c Watch a trailer for the sequel documentary Gore made in 2017. How does the main message make you feel? Watch again and do the tasks.

1. List the visual images chosen to illustrate the effects of global warming and discuss their impact on you.

   _____
   _____

2. Explain what happened in Paris in 2015 and why it was so important.

   _____

3. Point out what you find encouraging in Gore's message.

   _____

d Talk about a prediction Gore made in his first film and how it was justified by subsequent events.

Practice: Getting our future back

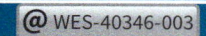

12 Kids Against Plastic

a Read this article and complete it with the letters A – J for the phrases below.

A home-schooled by their parents
B on a family trip
C before it is too late for the planet
D and in the ocean
E and not so young people
F as part of a project assignment
G to reduce plastic waste
H two British sisters
I when they were 12 and 10 years old
J and even councils

Kids Against Plastic is a youth-led organization founded by _____ (1), Amy and Ella Meek _____ (2). The organization aims to raise awareness about the impact of plastic on the environment and encourage young people _____ (3) to take action against plastic pollution _____ (4).

The two sisters _____ (5), began their crusade against single-use plastic while studying the UN Global Goals for Sustainable Development _____ (6). When Amy and Ella went to Indonesia _____ (7), they were shocked by the amount of plastic waste they saw on the beaches _____ (8). Since then, they have been tireless advocates for the environment. The girls have campaigned against other forms of plastic pollution and have organized large litter pick-up schemes for schools. They also help schools, businesses and festivals _____ (9) become 'Plastic Clever'.

In 2018, Amy and Ella Meek were named 'Activists of the Year' at the UK National Diversity Awards. They have also been recognized by the UN for their work _____ (10).

b Use the conjunctions in the box to complete the text by a climate activist.

> although ■ as (2×) ■ as soon as ■ before ■ if (3×) ■ unless

Climate change, a pressing global concern, demands immediate action. The consequences will be dire _____ (1) we fail to address it. _____ (2) rising temperatures and extreme weather events are becoming more frequent, ecosystems and communities are suffering irreparable damage. _____ (3) ice sheets melt and sea levels rise, coastal regions face catastrophic flooding. _____ (4) climate change is affecting agriculture and causing food scarcity, its significance is still not fully recognized by everyone. _____ (5) we continue on our current route, the situation will worsen. _____ (6) we transition to sustainable practices,

continued on page 64

future generations will suffer for our inaction. We must act _____ (7)
10 irreversible tipping points are reached. _____ (8) governments, industries, and individuals truly collaborate, we can mitigate the crisis. _____ (9) we recognize the importance of preserving our planet, we can work in unity to secure a healthier future for all.

13 VIEWING FOCUS: *Worse than I thought*

a Stella Bowles is a Canadian environmentalist, author and the youngest recipient of the Order of Nova Scotia. She co-wrote a book for children called *My River: Cleaning up the LaHave River*. She gave a TEDx talk about her project entitled *Oh poop! It's worse than I thought*. Watch the first part of the video (01:17 – 04:55) and decide if the following statements are true or false. Correct the false ones.

		True	False
1	Stella's great-grandfather installed a septic system seven years ago.	☐	☐
2	The septic system collapsed because it was being used less.	☐	☐
3	The gentleman who assessed the situation told Stella's mother they had six months to fix the septic system.	☐	☐
4	Stella's mother was angry that their neighbours were flushing their sewage directly into their river.	☐	☐
5	Stella's first science fair project was about septic systems.	☐	☐
6	A straight pipe is a pipe from a home's toilet directly into a waterway with no filtration.	☐	☐
7	Stella's parents got in contact with a local organization called Coastal Action Foundation.	☐	☐
8	Stella tested the water in the Le Havre River for faecal bacteria in a laboratory.	☐	☐

b Watch the second part of the video (05:05 – 06:18) and do the tasks.

1 Say why stirring up the bottom of the water is bad.

2 Outline what happens if you swim in the water with a reading of 70.

3 Say how much water is used to make the next sample easier to count.

4 Explain how to calculate the number of dots in the sample.

5 Summarize why you should not swim in the town bridge water.

6 Outline how many colonies of faecal bacteria would require the whole process to be redone.

7 Say why it is important to sterilize equipment before testing.

8 Explain the purpose of doing a control when testing.

Workshop 3

→ students' book, pages 100/101

@ WES-40346-003

c Watch the final part of the video (06:20 – 08:50) and choose the correct answer(s).

1. What is the recommended depth for swimming in the river?
   - [ ] a 70
   - [ ] b 100
   - [ ] c 170
   - [ ] d 200

2. Is it safe to swim in the LaHaye River?
   - [ ] a Yes, it is safe.
   - [ ] b No, it is not safe.
   - [ ] c It depends on the season.
   - [ ] d It depends on the time of day.

3. Why did Stella want to warn people about the river?
   - [ ] a Because it is too deep.
   - [ ] b Because it is too cold.
   - [ ] c Because it is contaminated with faecal bacteria.
   - [ ] d Because it is too polluted.

4. How did Stella initially plan to warn people about the river?
   - [ ] a By putting up a big sign.
   - [ ] b By creating a Facebook page.
   - [ ] c By telling her friends and family.
   - [ ] d By calling the media.

5. Why did Stella's mother initially refuse to let her create a social media page?
   - [ ] a Because she was too young.
   - [ ] b Because she didn't have enough followers.
   - [ ] c Because her mother didn't like social media.
   - [ ] d Because her mother didn't think it would make a difference.

6. What did Stella do to make their social media posts more positive?
   - [ ] a She included scientific facts.
   - [ ] b She only posted pictures.
   - [ ] c She asked her mother for help.
   - [ ] d She ignored negative comments.

7. What did Stella do to back up her scientific findings?
   - [ ] a She went to a lab and did testing.
   - [ ] b She asked their friends for help.
   - [ ] c She read articles online.
   - [ ] d She went to a conference.

8. What did Stella's project lead to?
   - [ ] a A clean-up plan for the river.
   - [ ] b A new swimming pool.
   - [ ] c A new park along the river.
   - [ ] d A new school.

9. Who came together to create the clean-up plan for the river?
   - [ ] a Stella and her family.
   - [ ] b The local community only.
   - [ ] c All three levels of government.
   - [ ] d Environmental organizations only.

Assessing claims

14 Reliability of sources

a You have been asked to write a report on teenagers' spending habits today. You do some research online and find these sources. Read them, then do the tasks.

A [...] Teens nowadays are aware of brands and social media, and they constitute a significant portion of the population that spends a significant portion of their earnings on clothing, food, footwear, cellphones, video games, and other items. [...]
Teenage girls and boys spend the majority of their money on clothes and accessories. They are establishing their own unique style, and as they reach adolescence, they are more adventurous with their wardrobe choices.
Teenagers spend most of their money on food, which is the second most expensive category [...].
Aside from the two major expenditures stated above, teenage females spend a lot of money on cosmetics, while teenage boys spend a lot of money on video games.
https://www.renolon.com/teenage-spending-statistics/

B What do American teens spend money on?
• Clothing accounts for 21% of the teens' budget (highest).
• Second highest is food is (20% of overall spending).
• Upper income teens spend on clothes adds up to nearly $1,100 annually.
• 10% of teens' budget is spent on shoes.
• Over 50% of all teens shop from online retailers.
• 83% of all teens have a smartphone and use it to shop with it.
https://www.renolon.com/teenage-spending-statistics/

C How much money does the average teenager spend?

Last updated March 25

[...] The majority of teenage spending goes towards food and clothing, constituting 42% of overall expenditures. This is the first time teens spent as much on food as they did on clothing. Twenty-six percent of teenage girls and 47% of teenage boys preferred online shopping; these numbers are higher than in previous years. The average income for teens is $2,767 for those in the 12 to 14-year-old range, and $4,923 for teens between 15 and 17 years old.
https://www.reference.com/world-view/much-money-average-teenager-spend-3fbb309f1fdb12af

1 Assess the claims in each source: Copy and fill in the table. <u>Underline</u> or (circle) relevant parts to support your findings.

	relevant	accurate	time-specific	country-specific
...				

2 Use your table in **1** to write one or two sentences about which source you find the most reliable and why. What are the shortfalls?

b Do some research about German teenagers' spending habits today. Assess your sources and write a brief report (180 words), acknowledging the shortcomings of your sources.

Back to the future

15 **Big Brother is watching you!**

a Watch the video and do the tasks.

1 List some common themes in dystopian movies.
   _____

2 Say how dystopian movies typically depict power structures.
   _____

3 Describe what motivates the protagonists in dystopian movies.
   _____

4 Explain how dystopian worlds are typically visualized.
   _____

b Do some research and outline some potential reasons for the popularity of dystopian movies. Then summarize what the popularity of dystopian movies says about our society.

16 *Never let me go.* One of the films that features in the video is *Never let me go*, which is based on Nobel Prize winner Kazuo Ishiguro's novel. Read the review and do the tasks on page 68.

Never Let Me Go by Kazuo Ishiguro is a haunting and beautiful novel that explores the themes of love, loss, identity and the human condition. Set in an alternate version of England in the late 1990s, the story follows Kathy H., Ruth
5 and Tommy, three young friends who grow up together in an idyllic English boarding school called Hailsham.
As they grow older, the three friends begin to discover the dark truth behind their existence. They are clones created for the sole purpose of providing organ donations to non-clones,
10 known as 'normals'. The story is narrated by Kathy H., who is now thirty-one years old and working as a carer for other clones who are in their final stages of organ donation. As she reflects on her past, she recalls Hailsham, where she and her friends were raised in an isolated environment, sheltered from the outside world.
15 The novel's central question is not whether the clones are human or not, but rather what it means to be human in a world where one's destiny is predetermined. Despite the heavy subject matter, the novel is ultimately a story of love and friendship, and the lengths people will go in an effort to protect those they care about.
Never Let Me Go is a masterful work that will stay with readers long after they finish
20 the last page. Ishiguro has created a world that is familiar and unsettling, and his exploration of what it means to be human is thought-provoking and deeply moving.

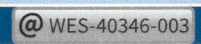

1 Say how the story is narrated, and who narrates it.
   _____
   _____

2 Describe what Hailsham is, and how it relates to the story.
   _____
   _____

3 Outline the central question of the novel, and why it is important.
   _____
   _____

4 Describe what themes the novel explores, and how they are related to the story.
   _____
   _____
   _____

17 What will be, will be

a Read this newspaper article about how younger generations envisage the future and complete it with the *will* future or future perfect form of the verbs in brackets.

As we look to the future, it's clear that the next generations _____ (1) (*face*) significant challenges. Among the most pressing are climate change, war and pandemics. However, there is also hope for a brighter future, and it's up to the young people of today to take action to create it.

In the coming years, climate change _____ (2) (*continue*) to be a major concern. The world is already experiencing the effects of global warming, with rising sea levels, extreme weather events and biodiversity loss. These problems _____ _____ (3) (*not get*) any better unless we take immediate action. By 2050, it is estimated that the world's population _____ (4) (*reach*) 10 billion, placing even greater strain on the planet's resources. It is clear that we _____ _____ (5) (*need*) to lead the way in reducing emissions, transitioning to renewable energy, and promoting sustainable lifestyles.

continued on page 69

The COVID-19 pandemic showed us how vulnerable we are to the spread of infectious diseases. The next generations _____ (6) (*have to*) be prepared to respond quickly and effectively to outbreaks, working together to limit their spread and find new treatments.

Despite these challenges, there is reason for hope. We _____ (7) (*not solve*) all of the problems by 2050, but we _____ (8) (*develop*) new technologies, explored new frontiers, and made progress in fields such as medicine, renewable energy and artificial intelligence. By that time, the young people of today _____ (9) (*reach*) positions of responsibility, and I hope we _____ (10) (*be*) at the forefront of these changes, driving innovation and finding solutions to the challenges we face.

b Write a paragraph about your hopes, plans and challenges for the future. Use future tenses and suitable phrases, e.g. *I hope, I want to, I'm going to, I'm planning on, I'm looking forward to ….*

_____
_____
_____
_____
_____
_____

18 **Our future concerns us all, doesn't it?** Add the correct question tag to the end of each sentence. Choose the correct tense.

1 The world is facing a climate crisis, _____?
2 We need to act fast to reduce carbon emissions, _____?
3 We haven't done enough to address the issue of climate change, _____?
4 We should continue to follow safety guidelines, _____?
5 We must remain vigilant against future pandemics, _____?
6 The world is going to face more challenges in the future, _____?
7 There's no doubt that war causes immense suffering, _____?
8 At the moment, peace seems almost impossible to achieve, _____?
9 Some people feel climate activists go too far with their protests, _____?
10 It is never easy to reach an agreement at COP, _____?

sixty-nine **69**

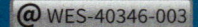

Practice: Speaking out

19 Speakers' Corner

a Look at the photo of Speakers' Corner in Hyde Park, London. Write a text about what you think happens there.

b Listen to a tourist guide explaining what Speakers' Corner is and its significance. Then do the tasks.

1. Explain what Speakers' Corner is.
2. Describe who the 'soapbox orators' are.
3. Say when Speakers' Corner started and why.
4. List some of the notable figures who have spoken at Speakers' Corner.
5. Explain why it is said that Speakers' Corner is inclusive.
6. Outline how Speakers' Corner differs from social media in the digital age.

20 Freedom of speech

a Read the article and complete it with the words and phrases from the box.

> in conclusion ■ in recent times ■ on the one hand ■ on the other hand ■ that is enshrined ■ they believe that ■ to silence dissenting voices ■ ultimately

Freedom of speech is a fundamental human right _____ (1) in many countries' constitutions. It is the idea that individuals should be able to express their opinions and ideas without fear of censorship or punishment. _____ (2), there has been an ongoing debate about whether there should be limits to this freedom. _____ (3), some argue that freedom of speech should be absolute. They believe that any attempt to limit it is a violation of individual rights and can lead to a slippery slope where governments can use censorship _____ (4). They also argue that allowing controversial or offensive speech is necessary for progress and social change. _____ (5), some people maintain that there should be limits to freedom of speech. _____ (6) hate speech, incitement to violence and defamation should not be protected under the guise of free speech because such speech can lead to discrimination and violence. So where do we draw the line? Should we allow individuals to say whatever they want or should we limit certain types of speech in order to protect people from harm? _____ (7), the answer is not clear-cut. Different societies will have different values and priorities when it comes to freedom of speech. Some may prioritize individual rights above all else, while others may prioritize social harmony and respect for diversity. It is up to each society to decide what balance to strike between these competing values. But, _____ (8), one thing is clear: freedom of speech is not an absolute right. It must be balanced against other important values such as equality, safety and respect for others.

b Find words in the text to match the definitions.

1 kept in a place that is highly admired and respected   _____
2 showing a strongly different opinion on a particular question   _____
3 causing disagreement or discussion   _____
4 encouraging someone to do or feel something unpleasant or violent   _____
5 obvious without needing any proof   _____
6 decide which of a group of things are the most important   _____

21 Social media and freedom of speech

a Complete these sentences about social media and freedom of speech with question tags.

1 Cyberbullying and harassment are common issues on social media, _____?
2 Only famous people experience cyberbullying and trolling on social media, _____?
3 Social media has the potential to be a powerful tool for free speech, _____?
4 We should be aware of the effects of social media and take a stand against harassment, _____.
5 Social media seems to bring out the worst in some people, _____?
6 Together, we can create a safer and more respectful online environment for everyone, _____?

b Listen to two teenagers and decide if the statements are true or false. Correct the false ones.

		True	False
1	J.K. Rowling faced harassment on social media after expressing her views on gender identity.	☐	☐
2	People engaged in a respectful discussion with J.K. Rowling despite disagreeing with her opinions.	☐	☐
3	The anonymity provided by social media platforms discourages hate speech and harmful rhetoric.	☐	☐
4	Treating others with respect and kindness is important on social media, even when we disagree with them.	☐	☐
5	It is not necessary for individuals to use social media responsibly and promote respect and civility online.	☐	☐
6	Creating a safer and more respectful online environment requires individual effort and collective action.	☐	☐

22 An essay on social media

a One of the teenagers you have just heard speaking wrote an essay about social media. Put the paragraphs in the right order and give the essay a title.

_____

A In conclusion, while social media has the potential to be a powerful tool for free speech and open dialogue, it is important to recognize the negative effects it can have on individuals and society as a whole. It is up to each of us to use social media responsibly and promote a culture of respect and civility online.

B As I have pointed out, social media has become a ubiquitous part of modern life, allowing people to connect with others and share their thoughts and opinions on a global scale. However, there is growing concern that social media has become a 'toxic form of gang rule', where individuals are subjected to online abuse and harassment for expressing their views.

C Moreover, social media algorithms often create echo chambers, where users are only exposed to content that reinforces their existing beliefs and biases. This can lead to a lack of critical thinking and a failure to engage with opposing viewpoints.

D On the one hand, social media platforms provide a platform for free speech and open dialogue, giving individuals the opportunity to express themselves and engage in important conversations about issues that matter to them. Social media has been instrumental in raising awareness about social justice issues and holding those in power accountable for their actions.

E However, there is also a dark side to social media. Many users have experienced cyberbullying, trolling and other forms of online harassment when expressing their opinions. The anonymity of social media allows people to say things they would never say face-to-face, leading to an increase in hate speech and harmful rhetoric.

1 _____ 2 _____ 3 _____ 4 _____ 5 _____

b Read the text again and do the tasks.

1 Describe some of the positive aspects of social media.
2 Outline some of the negative aspects of social media.
3 Summarize what echo chambers are and how they impact critical thinking and engagement with opposing views.
4 Say how the anonymity provided by social media contributes to an increase in harmful rhetoric and cyberbullying.
5 Explain what individuals can do to use social media responsibly and promote a culture of respect and civility online.

23 WRITING FOCUS: Under the influence.
Do some research about how teenagers at your school or in your city use social media. Write an article (200 words) and include the following points:
- what the teenagers use social media for
- how often do they use it
- which social media channels are most popular
- how much you think the teenagers are influenced by what they see online

World English

24 A dictionary history of English

a Read this article about two of the most famous dictionaries in English and choose the correct options to complete it.

Samuel Johnson's (1709 – 1784) ground-breaking *A Dictionary of the English Language* is one of the most famous English-language dictionaries in history. Published in 1755, it became the foremost English dictionary until the *Oxford English Dictionary* was published in the early 1900s.

In 1746, **some / lot of** (1) London booksellers commissioned Johnson to produce a dictionary of the English language. Over the next eight years, he scoured **a lot of / much** (2) books dating back to the 16th century. While Johnson's dictionary wasn't the first dictionary of the English language, no other dictionary had been so comprehensive: it has 42,773 entries and 140,871 definitions. **Each / A few** (3) word was defined in detail and included quotations from **many / much** (4) great writers, including Shakespeare. However, because he used books he liked, **much / most of** (5) the words used in the dictionary reflect Johnson's taste in literature.

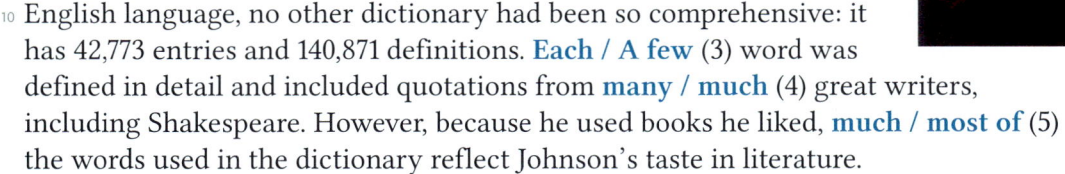

Johnson's dictionary also raised **a lot of / many** (6) criticism with critics saying that it included **some / any** (7) words and definitions that were considered questionable, the etymologies were flawed, and too **few / many** (8) of the definitions were skewed because of his biases and whims. Another big issue people had with his dictionary was that **several / any** (9) of the words he included were incomprehensible to the average reader.

In spite of **all / every** (10) these negative comments, it is undeniable that Johnson's dictionary had a significant impact on the English language. It helped standardize spelling and grammar and provided a reference point for future dictionaries. It would also influence the American *A Compendious Dictionary of the English Language* by Noah Webster, as well as the *Oxford English Dictionary*.

Noah Webster (1758 – 1843) believed passionately in the developing cultural independence of the United States. He advocated in particular a distinctive American language with its own idioms, pronunciation, spelling and style. **Many of / Much of** (11) the spellings that we associate with American English existed before Webster, but he championed them in his magnum opus, *An American Dictionary of the English Language*, published in 1828. It represented a new standard of lexicography. Webster's was a dictionary with 70,000 entries that was felt by **many / lots** (12) to be more authoritative than Samuel Johnson's 1755 British masterpiece. His dictionary contains seventy thousand words, **more / fewer** (13) than six thousand Bible references and remains one of the **more / few** (14) mainstream dictionaries to use Bible references to demonstrate the meaning of words. Webster was the first to document specifically American vocabulary such as *skunk*, *hickory* and *chowder*. He argued that **some / more** (15) spelling conventions were artificial and confusing, so he changed **many / few** (16) words, for example: *musick* to *music*, *centre* to *center*, and *plough* to *plow*.

Workshop 3

→ students' book, pages 108/109

b Find words in the text on page 73 to match the definitions.

1 very new and a big change from other things of its type _____

2 most important, leading _____

3 searched very carefully in order to try to find something _____

4 complete and including everything that is necessary _____

5 not perfect, or containing mistakes _____

6 not accurate or exact _____

c Explain the meaning of the following words.

1 bias _____
2 to champion _____
3 magnum opus _____
4 authoritative _____
5 masterpiece _____
6 mainstream _____

25 World English Editor

a Danica Salazar, the World English Editor for the *Oxford English Dictionary*, offers an insight into her work. Watch the first part of this video (00:00 – 01:23) and do the tasks.

1 Outline what Danica's job is and what it involves.
2 Describe Danica's particular focus when researching for the *Oxford English Dictionary*.
3 Say how people around the world adapt English words to express things in their local context.
4 Give an example of how a word or an expression has been adapted in the Philippines.
5 Explain why many houses in the Philippines have a 'dirty kitchen'.

b Watch the second part of the video (01:24 – 02:33) and complete these sentences.

1 Technological developments affect _____.
2 Oral language is harder to _____.
3 People write _____.
4 Many of the things that are posted on social media are _____.
5 Access to this hybrid written-oral genre is _____.
6 The OED is interested in _____.

c Watch the last part of the video (02:34 – 04:09) and do the tasks.

1 Say what the two meanings of 'chaebol' are and how they have evolved.
2 Say what the OED is doing with World English words.
3 Explain why Danica enjoys working on World English words for the OED.
4 Outline what she means by 'a little window into the everyday realities of English speakers all over the world'.

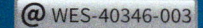

Practice: Broadening your horizons

26 Helpful advice. Listen to Rollo and Natasha and do the tasks.

1. Say what the conversation is about.
2. Outline the advantages of going on an Erasmus programme.
3. Explain how living in a foreign country can help you develop a global perspective.
4. Describe what challenges students can face during their Erasmus experience.
5. Explain how universities support students who participate in Erasmus.
6. Summarize why language barriers might be challenging.

27 My Erasmus experience

a Natasha has written a blogpost about her Erasmus experience. Read the blogpost and give each paragraph a title.

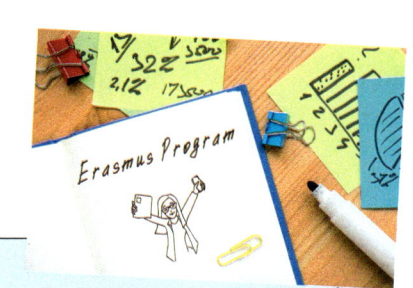

_____

Stepping out of my comfort zone and **embarking** on an Erasmus programme has been one of the best decisions I have made in my life. It provided me with an opportunity **to broaden my horizons**, explore new cultures and forge lifelong friendships. Today, as I reflect upon my Erasmus journey, I can proudly say that, despite a few challenges along the way, this experience has shaped me into a more **resilient**, adaptable and globally conscious individual.

_____

During my initial days, I was admittedly nervous and excited all at once. As I set foot into the university campus, I was greeted by a warm and diverse community of students from across the globe. Together, we shared a common goal: to immerse ourselves in a new culture, acquire knowledge, and create memories to last a lifetime. Our shared enthusiasm for learning and adventure acted as a **catalyst** for incredible friendships to **blossom**.

15 _____

Although I was engrossed in the wonders of my host city, my studies were equally important to me. The academic environment was stimulating and **intellectually fulfilling**. The classroom discussions, thought-provoking lectures, and research opportunities broadened my perspective and **nurtured** my intellectual curiosity.

20 _____

However, my Erasmus experience was not without its fair share of challenges. Language barriers initially posed a **hurdle** but, with time and perseverance, I overcame them and developed a working proficiency in the local tongue. Adjusting to a different educational system, new academic requirements, and the pressure to succeed in an unfamiliar environment was difficult. Yet, with resilience and the support of my fellow international students, I emerged stronger and more self-assured.

continued on page 76

As weeks went by, I found myself becoming more proficient in Spanish. Immersing myself in the local language was a vital part of my cultural integration and a way to connect
30 with the local community on a deeper level. Conversing with locals in their native tongue allowed me to delve into their traditions, customs and ways of life, making me feel like a citizen of the world.

My Erasmus experience has been a transformative adventure, shaping my perspective
35 on the world and my place within it. The friendships **forged**, the cultural immersion, and the academic challenges have all contributed to my personal and professional growth. To anyone contemplating an Erasmus programme, I **wholeheartedly** encourage you to seize the opportunity and embark on this life-changing journey. It will undoubtedly be an experience of a lifetime.

b Explain the meaning of the words and phrases in **bold** in your own words.

1 embarking
2 resilient
3 to blossom
4 nurtured
5 forged
6 to broaden my horizons
7 catalyst
8 intellectually fulfilling
9 hurdle
10 wholeheartedly

c Answer the questions.

1 How does Natasha describe her initial feelings as she began her Erasmus journey?

2 Besides cultural immersion, what other aspects of the academic environment did she find stimulating?

3 What were the initial challenges Natasha faced during her Erasmus journey?

4 What role did language proficiency play in Natasha's cultural integration and connection with the local community?

28 READING FOCUS: Study programmes around the world

a Read the leaflet on page 77 about study programmes in Canada and complete it with letters A–G for the sentences below.

A International students can only work up to twenty hours per week during the regular academic term but can work more frequently during the holidays.
B A world-class university system, high living standards, a strong job market and a friendly society make Canada a popular study-abroad destination.
C Students who work part-time in Canada earn an average of CAD 42,565 per year.

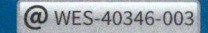

D Historically, Canada has been a welcoming country for immigrants from all over the world.
E As a result, Canadians pride themselves on being reasonable, polite and inclusive, making them natural leaders.
F Education quality rivals that of the United States and the United Kingdom, but tuition costs and living expenses are considerably lower.
G Home to 388,782 international students, Canada is always a promising prospect for education.

Ultimate Guide to Studying in Canada

Canada is serious about education; its universities demonstrate that commitment with beautiful ultra-modern campuses. _____ (1).

_____ (2). Several degree programmes are available in Canada, ranging from humanities to technology and health, as well as some specialized environmental programmes that are only available here.

There are also many English and French language schools that offer a variety of extracurricular activities, such as skiing and camping. _____ (3). As an international student, your lifestyle and spending habits will determine your cost of living in Canada. The average cost of living for a student in Canada is CAD 1,202 per month without rent.

One of the most beneficial things about being an international student in Canada is getting a part-time job to help alleviate living and studying costs. _____ (4).

Getting a part-time job requires you to be enrolled as a full-time international student, meaning you'll need a valid study permit; secondly, you can start working once your studies begin, not before. Once you graduate, you can seek a work permit to continue working. _____ (5). You can work as a tutor, barista, dog walker, sales assistant, or delivery driver.

Canada's culture is characterized by its tolerance, respect and community-oriented approach. Despite being individually oriented, Canadians value and emphasize community contributions. _____ (6).

_____ (7). Immigrants can expect to interact and integrate with multicultural communities, something that can make a big difference in making you feel comfortable in your new environment at first.

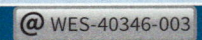

b Read the leaflet on page 77 again and choose the correct answer.

1 What makes Canada a popular study-abroad destination?
- [ ] a Its world-class university system
- [ ] b Its high living standards
- [ ] c Its strong job market
- [ ] d All of the above

2 What types of degree programmes are available in Canada?
- [ ] a Only humanities and technology
- [ ] b Only health and environmental programmes
- [ ] c Humanities, technology, health and some specialized environmental programmes
- [ ] d Only English and French language programmes

3 What is one of the most beneficial things about being an international student in Canada?
- [ ] a The ability to work part-time to alleviate living and studying costs
- [ ] b The ability to study for free
- [ ] c The ability to travel for free
- [ ] d The ability to receive free healthcare

4 When can international students start working part-time in Canada?
- [ ] a Before their studies begin
- [ ] b Once they graduate
- [ ] c Once their studies begin
- [ ] d It is not mentioned in the text

5 What values characterize Canada's culture?
- [ ] a Tolerance and respect
- [ ] b Inclusivity
- [ ] c Community-oriented approach
- [ ] d All of the above

c Do some research to write a similar text about study programmes for foreign students in Germany.

_____
_____
_____
_____
_____
_____
_____
_____

Workshop 3

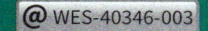

→ students' book, pages 112/113

@ WES-40346-003

Reporting on fake news

29 **The perfect solution!** Listen to a conversation between two friends. What are they talking about? Use some of these adjectives to describe their state of mind.

> calm ■ cautious ■ convinced ■ excited ■ gullible ■ interested ■ naïve ■ positive ■ relieved ■ sceptical ■ surprised

30 **It's the perfect solution, or is it?** Read the article the friends talk about. Underline or highlight parts that make you suspicious of the reliability of the article.

---

tips4teens.com **A scientific breakthrough – perfect body in less than a week**

It is a well-known fact that nowadays body image is more important to teenagers than ever before. Surveys show that lots of them have tried dieting, cutting out junk food or
5 doing exercise regularly, but found that the desired result is still nowhere in sight. If you are one of them, don't despair – there is a solution.
Scientists have come up with the perfect
10 supplement that works every time, for everyone, without giving up on your favourite snack or spending hours in the gym. All you need to do is take this brand-new supplement before you go to bed and watch the kilos melt away. Never in the history of weight management has there been a solution this easy. All you need to do is click on this link, get your supply and soon you'll be the envy of your friends. 'It's a miracle' says Moni who took the pills only
15 for five days. 'My friends can't believe how much my body shape changed in no time at all.'

---

31 **Checklist.** Look at the friends' checklist and write your comments or add the examples you marked in the article for each category.

_____
_____
_____
_____
_____

Checklist:
— website / URL
— claims / evidence
— style / language
— errors
— photos
— other observations
— author

32 **Assessing claims.** Summarize your assessment of the article. Write 150 – 200 words.

Mediation

33 Social media and young people. Together with your Canadian friend Parker, you are writing a weekly blogpost about social media. This week, you want to write about how younger people can be taught to use social media in a responsible way. You have come across this best-practice example in a German newspaper. Summarize it for Parker in English. Write about 150 words.

**Medienscouts in Mettmann –
Damit das Handy nicht zum Tatort wird**
[...]
Von Robert Ferdinand Krieger

Auch wenn das Internet kein Neuland mehr ist, bringt es aktuell mehr denn je Gefahren und Problematiken mit sich. Ob Verhaltensregeln in den sozialen Medien, Verletzungen von Persönlichkeitsrechten
5 oder die Sicherheit der eigenen Accounts [...]. Junge Menschen müssen den korrekten Umgang mit den sozialen Medien häufig erst lernen.
Dieser Herausforderung ist sich auch das Heinrich-Heine-Gymnasium in Mettmann bewusst. Bereits seit 2017 gibt es an der Schule deswegen sogenannte „Medienscouts".
[...]
10 Das Aufgabenfeld der Medienscouts ist vielfältig. So können Sie beispielsweise für Unterrichtsstunden gebucht werden. In dieser Unterrichtsstunde, [...] bringen die Expertinnen den Mitschülern die Welt des Internets näher. So wird beispielsweise das Thema „Recht am eigenen Bild" thematisiert. Schließlich kann ein Schüler nicht einfach ein Foto eines anderen posten, ohne dessen Einverständnis. „Auch wie man sichere
15 Passwörter im Internet erstellt und seine Privatsphäre auf den sozialen Medien wie Instagram verbessert und absichert, versuchen wir den Schülern beizubringen", erklärt Anna. Als präventive Maßnahme statten die Medienscouts den neuen Fünftklässlern einen Besuch ab, um auch die Jüngsten mit der Welt der sozialen Medien und deren Umgang vertraut zu machen.
20 Neben den Klassenbesuchen kann man die Medienscouts auch jederzeit in den Pausen auf dem Schulhof oder auch im eigenen Raum des Teams ansprechen. „Ein häufiges Problem ist das Zu-Spammen der WhatsApp-Klassengruppen mit Nachrichten und Stickern", schildert Paula. „Wir versuchen dann gemeinsam mit den Beteiligten Regeln für den Klassenchat aufzustellen. Das funktioniert dann auch eigentlich immer gut",
25 fährt sie fort. „[...] Ein großer Vorteil der Medienscouts ist der direkte Kontakt von Schüler zu Schüler, ohne dass ein Lehrer dabei ist. Das mache es den Betroffenen häufig einfacher sich zu öffnen, da die Gespräche auf Augenhöhe stattfinden.
Um überhaupt Medienscout zu werden, bedarf es einer sechsmonatigen Grundausbildung. „Diese Grundausbildung wird vom Land NRW finanziell unterstützt und
30 mitorganisiert", schildert Medienscout Mathilda. Aber auch nach der Grundausbildung bilden sich die Mettmanner Medienscouts fort. So besuchten sie im vergangenen Mai gemeinsam die „Bundesjugendkonferenz Medien" in Rostock. Hier konnte das Team in Workshops und Präsentationen wichtige Erkenntnisse für die Arbeit als Medienscout mitnehmen. „Besonders was das Thema künstliche Intelligenz angeht, konnten wir
35 einige interessante Dinge erfahren", findet Stella. „Auch der Austausch mit anderen

Workshop 3

→ students' book, pages 114/115

@ WES-40346-003

Medienscouts von anderen Schulen und Bundesländern war sehr interessant", erklärt Paula.

Unterstützt bei ihrer Tätigkeit als Medienscouts, werden die fünf Schülerinnen von den Lehrern Felix Laumen und Patrick Falcke. [...]

40 Das Feedback für die Arbeit der Medienscouts fällt durchweg positiv aus. Besonders die Eltern freuen sich über das Engagement der Medienscouts. „Die Eltern kennen sich schließlich häufig auch nicht so gut mit Instagram, TikTok und Co. aus, weshalb Sie froh sind, dass Ihren Kindern der korrekte Umgang in der Schule nähergebracht wird", erklärt Felix Laumen.

Source (abbreviated): Robert Ferdinand Krieger, „Damit das Handy nicht zum Tatort wird", Rheinische Post, 22.08.2023, https://rp-online.de/nrw/staedte/mettmann/social-media-medienscouts-lotsen-durch-digitale-welt_aid-95924225 [14.09.2023]

34 **The dangers of social media.** Your friend Parker has written a text about the dangers of social media and the effects they can have on people using them. Check that you understand all the terms he uses. Look at the points below and write a short evaluation in German of all the issues.

The utilization of social media platforms presents a range of significant dangers that have tangible and far-reaching impacts. Privacy breaches are a stark reality, as users' personal data is susceptible to unauthorized access and
5 exploitation. Cyberbullying and online harassment have become rampant issues, causing real emotional harm and even driving some individuals to extreme measures. Misinformation and fake news, amplified by the viral nature of social media, contribute to the spread of false narratives and hinder informed
10 decision-making.
Excessive social media use has been linked to addiction and negative effects on mental health, with users reporting feelings of isolation and decreased self-esteem. The curated nature of content on these platforms can foster unrealistic comparisons and contribute to mental health struggles. Additionally, social media's algorithms can inadvertently
15 create echo chambers, reinforcing existing beliefs and exacerbating societal divisions. Overall, the dangers of social media encompass concrete issues such as privacy violations, emotional harm, misinformation, addiction, mental health challenges, and the exacerbation of social divisions.

1 Datenschutz und Datenmissbrauch _____

2 Cybermobbing und Online-Belästigung _____

3 Falschinformation und Fake News _____

4 Auswirkungen auf die psychische Gesundheit und Sucht _____

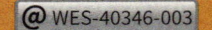

My review

1 About cultural identity
1. emigrated
2. was born
3. had insisted
4. was playing
5. heard
6. decided
7. knew
8. were constantly telling
9. practiced
10. started
11. had not learned
12. had grown up
13. found
14. had made
15. realized
16. felt
17. did not completely identify
18. travelled

2 About future solutions to environmental crises

a
1. climate
2. zero
3. fossil
4. emit
5. greenhouse
6. levels
7. energy
8. sustainable

b
1. am going to reduce, will take, taking part
2. won't be around, will have got
3. will look back, will be
4. won't have reached, are going to continue
5. won't be living
6. will have found, will ensure

3 About dystopian literature

a
1. d
2. a
3. c
4. g
5. b
6. h
7. e
8. f

b
1. wasn't it?
2. isn't it?
2. haven't you?
4. don't you?
5. don't they?
6. would they?

4 About expressing your opinion

a
1. it is evident
2. I admit
3. to sum up
4. we must remember
5. however
6. the main thing is
7. for a start
8. I believe

b
Possible answers:
1. I believe
2. However
3. For a start
4. It is obvious
5. In my opinion
6. it is important to consider
7. it is evident
8. Nevertheless
9. We must remember
10. In conclusion

Appendix

Grammatical terms

> Here are some of the most important **grammatical terms** in English:

active	aktiv
adjective	Adjektiv; Eigenschaftswort

adverb
    adverb of frequency
    adverb of manner
    adverb of place
    adverb of time
	Adverb (Wortart); Umstandswort
	    Adverb der Häufigkeit
	    Adverb der Art und Weise
	    Adverb des Ortes
	    Adverb der Zeit

adverbial	adverbiale Bestimmung (Satzglied); Umstandsangabe

article
    definite article
    indefinite article
	Artikel
	    bestimmter Artikel
	    unbestimmter Artikel

aspect	Aspekt
auxiliary	Hilfsverb

clause
    adverbial clause
    comment clause
    contact clause
    if-clause
    main clause
    relative clause
        defining relative clause
        non-defining relative clause
    subordinate clause (of time)
	Teilsatz
	    Adverbialsatz
	    nicht notwendiger Relativsatz, der sich auf den gesamten Satz bezieht
	    notwendiger Relativsatz ohne Relativpronomen
	    Bedingungssatz; Konditionalis
	    Hauptsatz
	    Relativsatz
	        notwendiger Relativsatz
	        nicht notwendiger Relativsatz
	    Temporalsatz

comparative	Komparativ; Vergleichsform

conditional / *if*-sentence
    conditional / *if*-sentences type 1, 2, 3, mixed
	Konditionalis; Konditionalsatz
	    Konditionalsatz Typ 1, 2, 3, gemischt

demonstrative determiner	Demonstrativbegleiter

future
    future with *going to*
    future with *will*
    present progressive with future meaning
    simple present with future meaning
    future progressive
    future perfect
	Futur; Zukunft
	    Futur mit *going to*
	    Futur mit *will*
	    Verlaufsform des Präsens mit Zukunftsbezug
	    einfache Form des Präsens mit Zukunftsbezug
	    Verlaufsform des Futur
	    Futur II

gerund	Gerundium
imperative	Imperativ; Befehlsform

infinitive
    to–infinitive
	Infinitiv; Grundform
	    to-Infinitiv

modal
    modal substitute
	Modalverb
	    Ersatzform eines Modalverbs

negative	negativ; verneinend

noun
    countable noun
    uncountable noun
	Substantiv; Nomen
	    zählbares Substantiv
	    nicht zählbares Substantiv

object
    direct object
    indirect object
	Objekt
	    direktes Objekt
	    indirektes Objekt

participle
    participle construction
    past participle
    perfect participle
    present participle
	Partizip
	    Partizipialkonstruktion
	    Partizip Perfekt
	    having + Partizip Perfekt
	    Partizip Präsens

passive
    by-agent
	Passiv
	    Handelnde(r) im Passivsatz

past
    simple past
    past progressive
	Präteritum; Vergangenheit
	    einfache Form der Vergangenheit
	    Verlaufsform der Vergangenheit

past perfect
    past perfect
    past perfect progressive
	Plusquamperfekt
	    einfache Form des Plusquamperfekts
	    Verlaufsform des Plusquamperfekts

plural	Plural; Mehrzahl
positive	positiv; bejaht
possessive *'s*	*s*-Genitiv
possessive determiner	Possessivbegleiter

preposition
    preposition of place
    preposition of time
	Präposition
	    Präposition des Ortes
	    Präposition der Zeit

present
    simple present
    present progressive
	Präsens; Gegenwart
	    einfache Form des Präsens
	    Verlaufsform des Präsens

present perfect
    present perfect
    present perfect progressive
	Perfekt
	    einfache Form des Perfekt
	    Verlaufsform des Perfekt

pronoun
    indefinite pronoun
    interrogative pronoun
    object pronoun
    personal pronoun
    possessive pronoun
    reciprocal pronoun
    reflexive pronoun
    relative pronoun
    subject pronoun
	Pronomen
	    Indefinitpronomen; unbestimmtes Pronomen
	    Interrogativpronomen; Fragepronomen
	    Objektpronomen
	    Personalpronomen
	    Possessivpronomen; besitzanzeigendes Pronomen
	    Reziprokpronomen
	    Reflexivpronomen
	    Relativpronomen
	    Subjektpronomen

prop word *one/ones*	Stützwort *one/ones*
quantifier	Numeral; Zahlwort

question
    question tag
	Frage
	    Frageanhängsel; Bestätigungsfrage

reported speech
    backshift
	indirekte Rede
	    Rücksetzung der Zeitform um eine Stufe

singular	Singular; Einzahl
statement	Aussagesatz
subject	Subjekt
superlative	Superlativ
tense	Zeitform

verb
    regular verb
    irregular verb
	Verb; Tätigkeitswort
	    regelmäßiges Verb
	    unregelmäßiges Verb

word order	Wortstellung

Grammar

> Do you have a question about grammar?
> The **grammar appendix** explains all the grammar that you have learned and revised in this book.
> You can also watch the grammar videos which explain the most important grammar:
> Tenses (Present and perfect tenses, Video 16; Past tenses, Video 21; Future tenses, Video 24)
> The passive (Video 3)
> Reported speech (Video 4)
> Gerunds and infinitives (Video 7)
> *If*-sentences (Type 1 and 2, Video 10; Type 3, Video 14)
> You can find the grammar videos under the webcode for your students' book.

G 1	Tenses	WS 2/WS 3
G 1.1	Present tenses	WS 2
G 1.2	Past tenses	WS 3
G 1.3	Future tenses	WS 3
G 2	The passive	WS 1
G 3	Reported speech	WS 1
G 3.1	Reported speech in statements and questions in the present, present perfect and future	WS 1
G 3.2	Reported speech in statements and questions in the past and in requests, offers, orders and advice	WS 1
G 3.3	Changes to adverbs of time and place in reported speech	WS 1
G 4	Gerunds and infinitives	WS 1
G 5	*If*-sentences	WS 1/WS 2
G 5.1	*If*-sentences type 1	WS 1
G 5.2	*If*-sentences type 2	WS 1
G 5.3	*If*-sentences type 3	WS 2
G 5.4	Mixed types of *if*-sentences	WS 1
G 6	Relative clauses	WS 2
G 7	Modals	WS 2
G 7.1	Modal substitutes	WS 2
G 8	Conjunctions with time clauses	WS 3
G 9	Question tags	WS 3
G 10	Quantifiers	WS 3

Appendix

GRAMMAR

G 1 Tenses

G 1.1 Present tenses
Workshop 2

Simple present:
- The simple present is the infinitive of the verb without *to*. For the third person singular (*he / she / it*) we add *-s*. We make negatives and questions with a form of *do*.
  She **wants** to read the book.
  They **don't go** to the cinema very often.
  Who **does** this dog **belong** to?

- We don't use a form of *do* when the question word is the subject of the sentence.
  Who **helps** you if you have problems with your homework?

- We use the simple present to talk about something that happens all the time or that is always true.
  My mum **works** as a nurse.
  I **love** my dog.
  We normally **watch** football on Saturday afternoon.

Present progressive:
- We form the present progressive with *am / are / is + -ing*. We form the negative with *am not / aren't / isn't + -ing*. For questions, we put the subject between *am / are / is* and the *-ing* form.
  They**'re playing** tennis now.
  He **isn't working** today.
  What **are** you **doing**?

- We use the present progressive to talk about what is happening now while we are speaking.
  We **aren't eating** lunch at the moment.
  Are you **reading** that comic or can I have it?

- Some verbs do not have a progressive form, for example *know, like, want* or *understand*.

G 1.2 Past tenses
Workshop 3

Simple past:
- With regular verbs, we add *-ed* to the infinitive of the verb to make the simple past. We form the negative with *didn't* and questions with *did*.
  They **played** a concert in Glasgow yesterday.

- Some verbs don't add *-ed* in the simple past. They are irregular (see the list on **pages 103 – 105**).

- We use the simple past to talk about things that happened at a time in the past. We often use expressions of time like *yesterday, last Thursday, two months ago*, etc.
  We **stayed** in Canada for four weeks last summer.
  We **arrived** in the middle of a heatwave.
  We **didn't want** to leave – it **was** a great holiday!
  What similarities **did** you **find** between Canada and the USA?

Past progressive:
- We form the past progressive with *was / were + -ing*. We form the negative with *wasn't / weren't + -ing*. For questions, we put the subject between *was / were* and the *-ing* form.
  My parents met when they **were living** in Vancouver.
  Sorry, I **wasn't listening**. What did you say?
  Were the others **waiting** when you arrived?

Appendix

GRAMMAR

- We often use the past progressive together with the simple past to give background information.
  It **was raining** when I got up.
  While we **were cycling** home from training last week, I had an accident and fell off my bike.
  Jack went home from school early yesterday because he **wasn't feeling** well.
  What **were** you **doing** when I saw you in town last Saturday?

Present perfect:
- We form the present perfect with *has / have* + past participle. We form the negative with *hasn't / haven't* + past participle. For questions, we put the subject between *has / have* and the past participle.
  She **has called** several times.
  I **haven't spoken** to Chloe today.
  Have you **seen** this movie before?

- We use the present perfect in two main ways.
  - To talk about something in the past which is connected with or has consequences in the present. We often use the present perfect in this way with *yet* and *already*.
    I'**ve** already **booked** the tickets.
    I **haven't seen** the exhibition yet.
    Has she **given** her presentation yet?
  - To talk about something that started in the past and continues now. We often use the present perfect in this way with *for* and *since*.
    He'**s lived** in this house for ten years.
    We'**ve been** friends since we were seven.

Present perfect progressive:
- We form the present perfect progressive with *has / have* + *been* + *-ing*. We form the negative with *hasn't / haven't* + *been* + *-ing*. For questions, we put the subject between *has / have* and *been*.
  I'**ve been playing** the guitar for three years / since I was 11.
  We **haven't been playing** very well since our trainer left.
  How long **have** you **been learning** English?

- We often use the present perfect progressive to talk about an action or a situation which started in the past and continues to the present. We use it with *for*, *since* and *all* as well as in questions with *How long*.
  I'**ve been living** here for years / since 2022.
  The kids **have been playing** in the garden all afternoon.
  Sorry, I'm late. – Don't worry. We **haven't been waiting** long.
  How long **have** you **been working** here?

Past perfect:
- We form the past perfect with *had* + past participle. We form the negative with *hadn't* + past participle. For questions, we put the subject between *had* and the past participle.
  I was late and the exam **had** already **started**.
  He **hadn't told** me he was Meg's friend.
  Which travel guide **had** they **checked** before they left home?

- We use the past perfect to show that one event happened before another one in the past. We use the past perfect for the event that happened first and the simple past for the more recent event. We often use sequence adverbs such as *when, before, after* and *until* to link the two events.
  After we **had spent** 15 hours on a plane, we finally **arrived**.
  We **had hoped** to reach this place sooner, but the bad weather **slowed** us down.
  The boy **had** just **had** his 8th birthday when he **had** an accident and **died**.

- We also use the past perfect to show that something happened before a time in the past.
  We'**d travelled** over 200 miles by 12 o'clock.
  I **hadn't met** him before the concert last June.

Past perfect progressive:
- We form the past perfect progressive with *had + been + -ing*. We form the negative with *hadn't + been + -ing*. For questions, we put the subject between *had* and *been*.
  We'd been playing for 20 minutes when it started to rain.
  I hadn't been waiting for long when the bus came.
  Had you *been looking for* an internship for long before you got one?

- We use the past perfect progressive to focus on the length of the earlier action and to show that it was in progress before the second action started.
  I'd been playing rugby for three years when I became captain.
  We hadn't been driving for long when dad realized that he didn't have his phone.
  How long *had* the others *been waiting* when you finally arrived?

G 1.3 Future tenses
Workshop 3

Will-future:
- We form the *will*-future with *will* + the infinitive of the verb without *to*. The verb form always stays the same. For negatives we use *won't*. For questions we put the subject between *will* and the infinitive of the verb without *to*.
  I'm sure our neighbours **will help** us.
  They **won't be** on time.
  Will he **arrive** today?

- We use *will* to offer or promise to do something for somebody.
  I'll help you with your homework this evening.
  There isn't any milk in the fridge. – Don't worry. I **won't forget** to buy some this afternoon.

- We use *will* when we decide to do something spontaneously while we are speaking.
  You look hungry. **We'll buy** a sandwich.
  I'm so tired, I **won't stay up** much longer.

- We use *will* for predictions that are based on a personal feeling or an opinion.
  You'll love it in South Africa!
  It **won't take** long.
  It'll be more expensive than you think.

Going to-future:
- We form the *going to*-future with a form of *be* + *going to* + the infinitive of the verb without *to*. We make negatives with a negative form of *be*. For questions we put the subject between the form of *be* and *going to*.
  I'm going to work during the summer holidays.
  She'**s not going to win** the race.
  Are you **going to start** at a new school in September?

- We use *be + going to* for decisions and future plans that were made before the time of speaking.
  I'm going to join the school drama club next term.
  We're going to book our train tickets at the weekend.

- We use *be + going to* for predictions that are based on present evidence. In other words, there is something in the present that indicates something in the future.
  Look at the traffic. We'**re going to be** late.
  It looks like it'**s going to be** a lovely day.

Appendix

GRAMMAR

The simple present:
- We use the simple present to talk about future events when the statements are based on present facts, and when these facts are something fixed like a timetable, schedule or calendar. We use it with an expression of time.
  *The bus **leaves** at 6.30, please hurry up.*
  *The football match **starts** at three o'clock on Sunday.*

Present progressive:
- We use the present progressive to talk about future arrangements. Typically, we use it with an expression of time.
  *Next week, I**'m seeing** my cousin to discuss our holiday plans.*
  *We**'re meeting** at the pizzeria this evening.*
  *When **are** Isabella and Gabriel **going** to the US?*

Future perfect:
- We form the future perfect with *will have* + past participle. We make negatives with *won't*. For questions we put the subject between *will* and *have*. We often use the future perfect with *by*.
  ***Will** you **have had** dinner by 8.30?*

- We use the future perfect to talk about something already completed by a point in the future.
  *I**'ll have finished** my exams by the end of June.*

- We can use the future perfect to talk about something not completed by a point in the future.
  *I'm afraid I **won't have finished** my report by Friday.*
  *I **won't have had** time to do much research before the interview.*

Future progressive:
- We form the future progressive with *will be* + *-ing*.
  *Next year most of my friends **will be doing** an apprenticeship.*

- We use the future progressive for an action in progress at a specific time in the future.
  *Hopefully by September I**'ll be working** somewhere in the US or Canada.*
  *This time tomorrow, I**'ll be having** my final exam.*
  *At 3 o'clock, we**'ll be driving** to the airport.*

G 2 The passive   Workshop 1

Form:
- We form the passive with the appropriate form of *be* + past participle.
  *It is a story that **is told** to many children.*
  *The meeting **has been cancelled**.*
  *The book **was published** in 1997.*
  *The year 2020 **will be remembered** for the rise of the Black Lives Matter movement.*

- We form a question by putting the subject after the auxiliary verb *be* or between the auxiliaries if there are two of them.
  ***Is** the website **updated** every day?*
  *When **will** the museum **be opened**?*

- When a verb is followed by a preposition, the preposition stays in the same position in the passive.
  *We can make sure the place **is looked after**.*
  *At the hotel, all diets **are catered for**.*

eighty-nine **89**

- When a verb has two objects, the passive sentence can begin with either the direct or the indirect object. The direct object is usually a thing and the indirect object is usually a person. When we begin with the direct object, we use the preposition *to* or *for* before the indirect object.
  The land was given back **to the original owners**. OR **The original owners** were given back **the land**.
  Four seats were saved **for us**. OR **We** were saved **four seats**.

- Verbs that take two objects include: *ask, buy, find, get, give, lend, make, offer, pay, promise, sell, send, show, teach, tell*.

Use:
- We often use the passive when we do not mention who does an action, as we are more interested in what happens than who does it. This is usually because the person who does the action is obvious, unknown or not important. The passive also means we can avoid using vague subjects like *someone*, *people* and *they*.
  India **was divided** into two different countries.
  In the book, the animals escape and 'zoo law' **is replaced** by 'jungle law'.

- However, we can use the passive with *by* to say who does the action. This is often when we give new information about an existing topic. The passive enables us to put the existing information first and the new information second.
  The Mini **is owned by BMW**.
  The film **was directed by James Cameron**.
  In the past, India **was ruled by the United Kingdom**.

- We use *be* + past participle after modal verbs.
  Explain which of the stories **can be considered** true.
  You **won't be contacted** unless you give us permission.

- We use the passive infinitive *to be* + past participle after verbs that are normally followed by a *to*-infinitive (e.g. *allow, ask, expect, hope, like, need, want*).
  Write the items in your exercise book in the order you **expect** them **to be mentioned**.
  Racism is a topic that **needs to be addressed**.

- When we use the passive in a relative clause, we can sometimes omit the relative pronoun and *be*.
  She lives in a house (that was) **built** by her grandfather.
  This new illness, (which was) **discovered** by a doctor in Nigeria, has not been named yet.

The passive (all tenses) – Overview

Simple present (*am / is / are* + past participle)
The internet **is used** by billions of people every day.
Today, most goods **are paid for** electronically.

Simple past (*was / were* + past participle)
The match **wasn't won** by our team.
The mistakes **were corrected** by the teacher.

Present perfect (*has been / have been* + past participle)
Gwen **has been hired** by a fashion company.
Musical genres and fashion **have been linked** to young people since the 1920s.

Will (*will be* + past participle)
What kind of information do you think you **will be given**?
Many jobs **will be lost**.

Modal verbs (*can be / might be / had to be* + past participle)
Stories **can be used** to illustrate a point and appeal to the emotions of your audience.
The new website **might be launched** soon.
Until the early 20th century, all household chores **had to be done** by hand.

G 3 Reported Speech

G 3.1 Reported speech in statements and questions in the present, present perfect and future
Workshop 1

Statements:
- We can use *say* and *tell* to report what someone says.
  He **says** that he loves the area.
  Thomas **tells** me that you're going back to the UK.

- We can use *that* after *say* and *tell*. There is no rule about *that* and it is usually personal choice.
  She **says** she's not hungry.   OR   She **says that** she's not hungry.

- We use an indirect object (e.g. *me*, *us*) after *tell*.
  He tells **me** they are hoping to set off at about 6.30.

- As well as *say* and *tell*, we can use reporting verbs such as *admit, agree, assure, claim, deny, inform, suggest, think,* etc.
  He **admits** he's wrong.
  She **agrees** it's a good idea.

- When we use reporting verbs in the present, the present perfect or the future, we generally keep the information we are reporting in the same tense as the original comment. This is usually to show that something is still true, relevant or important.
  'I**'ll be** home in ten minutes.' → She says she**'ll be** home in ten minutes.
  'It**'s** Jenna's birthday today.' → Alice tells me it**'s** your birthday today.
  'I think Sam **left** about an hour ago.' → He thinks that Sam **left** about an hour ago.
  'We**'re going to** the beach.' → Luke says they**'re going to** the beach.

- We sometimes need to change pronouns (*we* → *they*).
  'I've lived in South India since **I** was 13.' → **He** says **he**'s lived in South India since **he** was 13.

Questions:
- We can report a question with verbs such as *ask*, *want to know* and *wonder*.
  Fred: 'Is everything OK?' → Fred**'s asking** if everything is OK.
  David: 'When are we leaving?' → David **wants to know** when we're leaving.
  Jessica: 'Where are we going next?' → She**'s wondering** where we are going next.

- For a *yes/no*-question (without a question word) we use *if* or *whether*.
  He **is asking** me **if** I know his brother.
  Olga **has asked** me **whether** I can give her a surfing lesson.

- The word order is different from direct questions but the same as in statements.
  'Where **does he live**?' → She wants to know where **he lives**.
  'When **are we leaving**?' → He keeps asking when **we're leaving**.
  NOT ~~She's wants to know where does he live.~~
  ~~He keeps asking when are we leaving.~~

G 3.2 Reported speech in statements and questions in the past and in requests, offers, orders and advice
Workshop 1

Statements and questions:

- When reporting speech, we often use the past tense forms *said, told, asked, wanted to know, was wondering, assured, admitted, denied, explained, promised, suggested*, etc. We usually 'backshift' the tense (move the tense one step back in time) in the statement, comment or question we are reporting.

present tense	→	past tense

'I **have** no time.' → She said she **had** no time.
'What's wrong with you?' → Keira asked Fred what **was** wrong with him.
'OK, I admit I'**m** wrong.' → He admitted he **was** wrong.

past tense / present perfect → past perfect
'I **didn't want** to go.' → She explained she **hadn't wanted** to go.
'We'**ve** just **arrived**.' → He said they'**d** just **arrived**.

will → would
'I'**ll call** you later.' → She promised she'**d call** me later.

can → could
'I **can't find** it.' → He admitted he **couldn't find** it.

must → had to
'We **must leave** now.' → She said they **had to leave**.

- We sometimes use the past tense forms of reporting verbs such as *said, told, asked, wanted to know, was wondering*, etc. and do not change the tense of the reported sentence. This is usually to show that a statement or information is still true, relevant or important.
  'Sam **left** about an hour ago.' → He said that Sam **left** about an hour ago.
  'I'**ll** be home in ten minutes.' → She said she'**ll** be home in ten minutes.
  'Where's Jamie **going**?' → She was wondering where Jamie'**s going**.

Requests, offers, orders and advice:

- We can report a request with verbs such as *asked* and *wanted* + indirect object + *to*-infinitive.
  'Can you wait here?' → She asked **us to wait** here.
  'Could you repeat the question?' → She wanted **me to repeat** the question.

- We can report an offer with *offer* + *to*-infinitive.
  'I can give you a lift if you like.' → Maria offered **to give** us a lift.
  'I'll help you if you like.' → He offered **to help** us.

- We can report an order or advice with *told* + indirect object + (*not*) + *to*-infinitive.
  'You should apologize to them.' → She told **me to apologize** to them.
  'Don't be late again.' → He told **me not to be** late again.

- We can also use the present tense of the reporting verbs:
  Gareth **wants** me **to help** him.
  She'**s asking** us **to wait** here.
  Petra'**s offering to give** us a lift.
  The life guard **is telling** us **not to swim** here.

G 3.3 Changes to adverbs of time and place in reported speech

Workshop 1

- When we are reporting with a reporting verb in the past, we need to change adverbs of time and place.
  'I saw Anders **yesterday**.' → She mentioned she'd seen Anders **the day before**.
  'I'll call you **next week**.' → She said she'd call me **the following week**.
  'This is the first time I've been **here**.' → He said it was the first time he'd been **there**.

- Common changes include:
  yesterday → the day before
  tomorrow → the next day / the day after
  last weekend / week / month / year → the weekend / week / month / year before
  next weekend / week / month / year → the following weekend / week / month / year
  here → there

G 4 Gerunds and infinitives

Workshop 1

Sometimes we use two verbs together. When one verb follows another verb, the second verb is usually a gerund (*-ing*) or a *to*-infinitive.

- We use the gerund (*-ing*) after certain verbs. These include: *admit, avoid, deny, don't mind, enjoy, feel like, finish, imagine, look forward to, mention, miss, practise, prefer, recommend, risk, suggest.*
  Many young people **enjoy travelling**.
  Have you **finished reading** the article?
  He **suggests doing** work experience at a law firm.

- We use the *to*-infinitive after certain verbs. These include: *arrange, choose, decide, expect, hope, intend, learn, manage, need, offer, plan, promise, want, would like.*
  She's **decided to study** music at university.
  Many young **want to volunteer** abroad.
  I'd **like to do** some kind of volunteer work.

- Some verbs can be followed by the gerund or the *to*-infinitive with no or little difference in meaning. These include: *like, love, hate, prefer, start.*
  I **hate getting up** early.   I really **hate to be** late.
  I **prefer doing** sport.   I **prefer to study** languages.

Some verbs can be followed by a gerund or the *to*-infinitive, but there is a difference in meaning. These include: *try, remember, forget, stop*.

- *Try:*
  We use *try* + gerund when we do something to see what the results will be.
  *I **tried turning** the computer on and off, but the programme still didn't work.*

  We use *try* + *to*-infinitive when we make an effort to achieve something.
  *I'm **trying to learn** Russian, but it's very difficult.*

- *Remember and forget:*
  We use *remember / forget* + gerund to talk about memories.
  *Do you **remember going** to school for the first time?*
  *I'll never **forget visiting** Prague. It's so beautiful.*

  We use *remember / forget* + *to*-infinitive to say we do or don't do something.
  *Did you **remember to email** Julia?*
  *Don't **forget to update** your CV!*

- *Stop:*
  We use *stop* + gerund to talk about something ending or stopping.
  *I **stopped eating** meat when I was 16.*

  We use *stop* + *to*-infinitive to express the reason or purpose.
  *I was working, but I **stopped to check** the news for a while.*

G 5 *If*-sentences

Workshop 1/Workshop 2

There are three types of *if*-sentences, as well as mixed types (→ G 5.4).

If-sentences type 1 → G 5.1
if-clause: simple present   main clause: *will* (*'ll*) + infinitive
*If I **go** to China,*   *I **will** / **'ll visit** the Great Wall.*
(= It's likely or possible that I'll visit China.)

If-sentences type 2 → G 5.2
if-clause: simple past   main clause: *would* (*'d*) + infinitive
*If I **went** to China,*   *I **would** / **I'd visit** the Great Wall.*
(= It's not very likely that I'll visit China.)

If-sentences type 3 → G 5.3
if-clause: past perfect   main clause: *would* (*'d*) + *have* + past participle
*If I **had gone** to China in 2019,*   *I **would have** / **I'd have visited** the Great Wall.*
(= I had the chance to go to China in the past, but I didn't go.)

Appendix
GRAMMAR

G 5.1 *If*-sentences type 1 *Workshop 1*

- We use *if*-sentences type 1 to talk about things that are possible or likely to happen.
  If-sentences type 1 have the form *if* + simple present, *will / won't* + infinitive.
  *If I **think** something's cool, I'**ll buy** it.*
  *If the phone **is** too expensive, I **won't buy** it.*
  *If I **need** some help, I'**ll message** you.*

- We use *unless* to mean *if not*.
  *We'll go for a walk **unless** it **rains**. = We'll go for a walk **if** it **doesn't rain**.*

- We use *when* for things which will definitely happen.
  ***When** I get home, I'll call you.*

- We can usually put the two clauses in any order. When the *if / when / unless*-clause is first, there is a comma between the clauses.
  *If I like it**,** I'll buy it.*
  I'll buy it if I like it.

G 5.2 *If*-sentences type 2 *Workshop 1*

- We use *if*-sentences type 2 to talk about things that are impossible or hypothetical in the present or unlikely to happen in the future.

- *If*-sentences type 2 have the form *if* + simple past, *would / wouldn't* + infinitive.
  *If I **got** a tattoo, my parents **wouldn't be** happy.*
  *If we **drove** less, there **wouldn't be** so much air pollution.*
  *If I **had** more money, I'**d buy** a new phone.*

  Note that we often use *'d* instead of *would*, especially in speaking and informal writing.

- We do not use *would* in the *if*-clause.
  *If I **had** more time, I'd read more books.* NOT ~~If I would have more time, I'd read more books.~~

- We can usually swap the order of the two clauses. When the *if*-clause is first, there is a comma between the clauses.
  *If I had more time**,** I'd read more books.*
  I'd read more books if I had more time.

- We can usually use *If I was …* or *If I were …* . However, we normally use *If I were you, …* .
  *If I **was / were** richer, I'd get a new car.*
  ***If I were you**, I'd work a bit harder at school.*

Note that we can use *could* or *might* in an *if*-sentence type 2.
*If I had more money, I **could buy** a new phone.*
*If we drove less, there **might not be** so much air pollution.*

G 5.3 *If*-sentences type 3

Workshop 2

- We use *if*-sentences type 3 to talk about something that didn't happen in the past. We talk about it in an imaginary or a hypothetical way.

- *If*-sentences type 3 have the form *if* + past perfect, *would / wouldn't have* + past participle.
  If I **had seen** you, I **would have said** hello.
  If I **had known** about the exhibition, I **would have gone** to it.
  If you**'d got up** earlier, you **wouldn't have missed** the bus.

- We often use *'d* instead of *had* and *would*, especially in speaking and informal writing. We also often use *'ve* instead of *have*.
  If I**'d had** more money, I**'d've got** a taxi.

- We can usually swap the order of the two clauses. When the *if*-clause is first, there is a comma between the clauses.
  If I'd had more money**,** I would've bought it.
  I would've bought it if I'd had more money.

Note that we can use *could have* or *might have* in an *if*-sentence type 3.
If I hadn't been ill last week, I **could have gone** to the meeting.
If I'd worked harder, I **might've got** better grades in my exams.

G 5.4 Mixed types of *if*-sentences

Workshop 1

- We use a 'mixed' *if*-sentence to talk about a past event with a present consequence. To do this we combine an *if*-sentences type 3 (to refer to the past) with an *if*-sentences type 2 (to refer to the present).
  If you **had gone** to bed earlier, you **wouldn't be** so tired now.
  If I**'d had** breakfast, I **wouldn't be** so hungry now.
  If he **hadn't had** those lucky breaks, no one **would know** his name today.
  If you**'d listened**, you**'d know** what to do!

Note that we can use *might* in a mixed *if*-sentence.
If you'd listened to the advice, you **might not be** in this mess now.

G 6 Relative clauses

Workshop 2

Relative pronouns:
- We use *who* for people and *which* for things. We can use *that* for both people and things. We use *whose* to show possession.

Defining relative clauses:
- A defining relative clause defines, identifies or gives necessary information about a person or thing.
- A defining relative clause comes immediately after this person or thing. The relative clause begins with a relative pronoun.
  There were basic human rights **which had been seriously curtailed**.
  It was a political situation **which arose after many years of oppression**.
  Nelson Mandela was not a man **who believed in or encouraged violence**.
  He and the others **who started the organization** were all arrested.

Omission of the relative pronoun:
- A relative pronoun can be the subject or the object of a relative clause.

	relative pronoun / subject	verb	object
There's the man	**who**	helped	us	yesterday.

	relative pronoun / object	subject	verb
There's the man	**who**	we	helped	yesterday.

- We can omit *who*, *which* or *that* when it is the object of the relative clause.
  Is this the book (which) your parents gave you as a birthday gift?
  Mac and his family do things (that) every other family does.
  Is this the café (that) Luke mentioned the other day?
  There's the man (who) we helped yesterday.

Non-defining relative clauses:
- A non-defining relative clause gives extra non-essential information about a person or thing. The non-defining relative clause comes immediately after this person or thing and begins with *who* or *which*, but not *that*. We always separate a non-defining relative clause from the main clause with commas.
  The African National Congress, **which was formed in 1912**, defended the rights of the African people.
  Mandela, **who was sentenced to life**, became the world's most famous prisoner.
  My two older brothers, **who I've always been very close to**, went to live with my dad.
  He was born in Avalon, **which is a small town near Los Angeles**.

Note that non-defining relative clauses are used more in writing and in more formal spoken contexts.

- We can also use a non-defining relative clause beginning with *which* to comment on the whole of the previous clause.
  I was at a party last weekend, **which was great fun**.
  The school became mixed-sex in the 1980s, **which was a major step forwards**.
  I missed the bus, **which was really annoying**.

Note that non-defining relative clauses used to comment on the whole of the previous clause are quite common in spoken and more informal English.

Where and *when*:
- We can use the relative adverbs *where* and *when* in relative clauses. We use *where* to identify a place and *when* to identify a time.
  *The hotel **where we stayed** is in the city centre.*
  *I can't remember a month **when we last had so much rain**.*

G 7 Modals

Workshop 2

The modal verbs are *can, could, must, might, may, would, will, shall* and *should*.

- A modal verb always has the same form. The ending never changes.
  *She **can** speak English.*

- We use an infinitive without *to* after a modal verb.
  *I **will** help you.*

- To form a negative, we put *not* or *n't* after the modal verb.
  *You **mustn't** do that.*

- To form a question, we put the modal verb before the subject.
  ***Can** you help me?*

Can and *could*:
We use *can* to talk about ability. We use it:
- to talk about general abilities and skills.
  *My sister **can** use many computer programmes.*
  *I **can** speak French and Spanish. But I **can't** speak Italian.*

- to talk about ability at a particular time.
  *I **can't** read this. The writing is too small.*

The past tense of *can* is *could*.
*I **could** speak some English when I was four years old.*

We use *can* to talk about permission. We use it:
- to talk about rules and laws and permission given by an individual.
  *You **can't** wear trainers at work. But you **can** wear jeans.*
  *You **can** leave when you have finished the report.*
  *We **could** wear trainers at work in my last job.*

We use *can* to talk about possibility.
*We **can** have the meeting on Thursday or Friday.*
*It **could** have been a rumour.*

May and *might*:
We use *may* and *might* to say that something is possible or likely. *Might* is more common in informal contexts. The negative is *may not* and *might not*. We use them:
- to say what is possible or likely in the future.
  *I **might** start looking for a holiday job.*
  *There **may** be a slight delay with your online order.*

- to say what we think is possible or likely in the present.
  *This **might** be Nina's office. But I'm not sure.*
  *She didn't answer the phone. She **might not** be at home.*

Appendix

GRAMMAR

Must:
We use *must* to talk about what is necessary or what is required. We use *must not* (or *mustn't*) to say that something is not allowed or forbidden.
You **must** come and visit us while you are in South Africa.
We **mustn't** forget the tickets.

Should:
We use *should* to make suggestions and give advice. The negative form is *shouldn't*.
They **should** check in online.
It **shouldn't** be a problem.

The past tense of *should* is *should have* + past participle.
We're going to be late – we **should have left** earlier.

Will and *shall*:
We use *will* in a number of ways. Note that *will* is often contracted to *'ll*. We use *will*:

- to express spontaneous decisions.
    I**'ll** help you if you want me to.
    I think I**'ll** take a short break.

- to express predictions or assumptions about the future, present or past.
    I'm hoping I**'ll** finish my essay by Friday.
    Hurry up! The taxi **will** be waiting.
    I think the exam **will** have finished by now.

- to talk about facts we see as inevitable or certain.
    I**'ll** be at school all day tomorrow.
    She**'ll** be 21 in January.
    We **will** see you tomorrow.

We mainly use *shall* in the form of a question to make offers and suggestions. We use it in this way with *I* and *we*.
Shall I help you?
What time **shall** we meet?

G 7.1 Modal substitutes

Workshop 2

Modal substitutes include: *be able to, have to, need to, be obliged to, ought to* and *be supposed to*.

Alternatives to *can* and *could*:
- We use *be able to* as an alternative to *can* and *could*. This is usually in more formal contexts and with *will* and the present perfect.
  Some people **are able to** speak several languages.
  I'm not able to fix the problem, I'm afraid.
  Unfortunately, I **wasn't able to** attend the event.
  He**'ll be able to** solve the problem.
  I**'ve been able to** speak English since I was four.

- We sometimes use *be allowed to* as an alternative to *can* and *could* to talk about permission.
  Are you **allowed to** use your phone for research in lessons?
  I **was** never **allowed to** stay up late on a school night.

Alternatives to *must*:
- We use *need to* and *have to* as alternatives to *must*. When they are used in this way, there is usually little difference in meaning (e.g. I **need to** prepare for my interview. / I **have to** prepare for my interview. / I **must** prepare for my interview.).
  They **need to** acknowledge this problem.
  You **need to** leave by 5.30 at the latest.
  Do you **have to** be there on Monday?

- In more informal contexts, such as conversation, we also use *have got to*.
  I**'ve got to** prepare for my exam.
  What time **have** we **got to** leave?

- The past tenses are *needed to* and *had to*. We use *had to* as the past tense of *must*.
  Sorry I'm late. I **needed to** stop at the shops on the way here.
  I **had to** stay at school later than usual today.
  He **had to** do an interview with the head teacher.

- We use *don't need to* and *don't have to* to say that something isn't necessary.
  We **don't need to** leave until midday.
  You **don't have to** drink that.

- We use *be obliged to* as an alternative in more formal contexts. This is usually when the obligation is a rule or law.
  You **are obliged to** report to the reception on arrival and when leaving the building.
  You **are not obliged to** give your private address.

Alternatives to *should*:
- We can sometimes use *ought to* as an alternative to *should* when we are making suggestions or giving advice.
  It **ought to** be easy now.
  You **ought to** wear a suit for the wedding.
  I think we **ought to** leave now.

- We use *be supposed to* as an alternative to *should* when we are expressing the correct thing to do.
  She **is supposed to** be back by lunch time.
  I**'m supposed to** go to New York next week.

G 8 Conjunctions with time clauses

Workshop 3

- We often use conjunctions such as *when, while, until, before, after, as soon as* and *once* to introduce an action that is going to happen in the future.

- When we are talking about the future, we usually use the simple present after a time conjunction.
  When I **think** of a way, I'll tell you.
  I'll let you know **as soon as** I **arrive**.

- We can also use the present progressive after a time conjunction to express that something is in progress.
  Let's meet **the next time** you**'re visiting** Berlin.

- We can also use the present perfect after a time conjunction to emphasize that one action is completed before the other action.
  When I**'ve finished** my presentation, I'll send it to you.

- When we begin with the time conjunction, we put a comma between the clauses.
  When we get to the station**,** I'll call you.
  I'll call you when we get to the station.

- We do not use a future form with *will* after the time conjunction.
  NOT ~~I'll call you as soon as I will arrive.~~
  ~~I'll email you when I will have time.~~

G 9 Question tags

Workshop 3

We form a question tag with an auxiliary verb (*do, have, be* or a modal verb) + pronoun (*you, he, she, it, they*, etc.). We use the same auxiliary verb as in the first part of the statement. For the simple present and simple past, we use a form of *do*.

We use a negative question tag after a positive statement.
We **seem** to have a great appetite for dystopia, **don't we**?
You **have** read older books than that, **haven't you**?

We use a positive question tag after a negative statement.
Science and technology **don't** help combat the climate crisis or anything, **do they**?
There **won't** be a problem identifying some of the dangers, **will there**?

We use a question tag in two main ways:
- when we expect someone to agree with us. In this case, the intonation on the question tag falls.

  I bet you got a good grade, **didn't you**?

  Online comments are largely anonymous, **aren't they**?

- when we ask a real question, often to check something. In this case, the intonation on the question tag rises.

  Your brother is still in the USA, **isn't he**?

  There was a movie too, **wasn't there**?

G 10 Quantifiers

Workshop 3

- We use quantifiers to express the quantity of something. Quantifiers are words such as *all, a few, a little, (hardly) any, both, each, every, most (of), neither, none, no, some, the whole of*.

- To talk about things / people in general, we use *all / most / many / some / a few / no* – plural noun or uncountable noun (without *the*).
  All children have the right to an education.
  Most countries have free education.
  Many people don't have a job.

- We can also use *no* + singular noun.
  Today, **no child** should go hungry.

- To talk about things / people in a specific group, we use *all / most / many / some / a few / one / none* + *of* + *the / my / their /* etc. + plural noun or uncountable noun.
  All of my friends were surprised.
  All of my work is interesting.
  One of his ambitions is to be a model.
  None of the jobs were interesting.

- We can also use *all / most / many / some / a few / one / none* + *of* + pronoun.
  Most of them have a summer job.
  A few of us are going to the meeting.

- We can also use *all* + *the / my / their /* etc. + plural noun or uncountable noun (without *of*).
  All my friends were surprised.
  I spend **all my allowance** on clothes.

- We use *each / every* + singular noun.
  I need to speak to **each person**.
  Every child has the right to express their opinion.

- To talk about two things, we use *both*. We use:
  - *both* + plural noun
    I like **both colours**.
    Both jobs were interesting.
  - *both (of)* + *the / my / these /* etc. + plural noun
    Both of the jobs were interesting.
    Both my parents speak English.
  - *both of* + pronoun
    Both of them are teachers.

- We use a number of other expressions with *of* + plural or uncountable noun / pronoun.
  The majority of people here don't have a passport.
  A large percentage of them have never travelled abroad.
  A lot of people didn't vote in the election.
  Three quarters of the land is used for farming.
  A third of the population lives in poverty.
  Thirty per cent of 18-year-olds go to university.
  Half of the country is desert.

- We usually use these expressions without *the* to talk about things / people in general, but with *the* to talk about specific groups.
  Over 50% of people don't have a passport.
  Over 50% of the people we interviewed don't have a passport.

Irregular verbs

infinitive	simple past	past participle	German
to arise [əˈraɪz]	arose [əˈrəʊz]	arisen [əˈrɪzən]	entstehen
to be	was / were	been	sein
to beat	beat	beaten	schlagen
to become	became	become	werden
to begin	began	begun	beginnen, anfangen
to bet	bet	bet	wetten
to bite [baɪt]	bit [bɪt]	bitten [ˈbɪtn]	beißen
to bleed [bliːd]	bled [bled]	bled [bled]	bluten
to blow	blew	blown	blasen
to break	broke	broken	brechen
to bring	brought	brought	bringen
to build	built	built	bauen
to burn	burnt / burned	burnt / burned	(ver)brennen
to burst	burst	burst	platzen
to buy	bought	bought	kaufen
to catch	caught	caught	fangen
to choose [tʃuːz]	chose [tʃəʊz]	chosen [ˈtʃəʊzən]	auswählen
to come	came	come	kommen
to cost	cost	cost	kosten
to cut	cut	cut	schneiden
to deal [diːl]	dealt [delt]	dealt [delt]	handeln
to dig	dug	dug	graben
to do [duː]	did [dɪd]	done [dʌn]	machen, tun
to draw	drew	drawn	zeichnen
to dream [driːm]	dreamt [dremt] / dreamed [driːmd]	dreamt [dremt] / dreamed [driːmd]	träumen
to drink	drank	drunk	trinken
to drive [draɪv]	drove [drəʊv]	driven [ˈdrɪvən]	fahren
to eat [iːt]	ate [et, eɪt]	eaten [ˈiːtn]	essen
to fall	fell	fallen	fallen, stürzen
to feed [fiːd]	fed [fed]	fed [fed]	füttern
to feel [fiːl]	felt [felt]	felt [felt]	(sich) fühlen, spüren
to fight	fought	fought	kämpfen
to find	found	found	finden
to fly	flew	flown	fliegen
to forget	forgot	forgotten	vergessen
to forgive	forgave	forgiven	vergeben
to freeze	froze	frozen	frieren
to get	got	got / gotten (AE)	bekommen, holen
to give	gave	given	geben, schenken
to go [gəʊ]	went [went]	gone [gɒn]	gehen, fahren
to grow [grəʊ]	grew [gruː]	grown [grəʊn]	wachsen, anbauen
to hang	hung	hung	hängen
to have (got)	had	had	haben
to hear [hɪə]	heard [hɜːd]	heard [hɜːd]	hören
to hide [haɪd]	hid [hɪd]	hidden [hɪdn]	(sich) verstecken
to hit	hit	hit	schlagen
to hold	held	held	halten
to hurt	hurt	hurt	wehtun

Appendix

IRREGULAR VERBS

infinitive	simple past	past participle	German
to **keep** [kiːp]	**kept** [kept]	**kept** [kept]	(be)halten
to **kneel** [niːl]	**knelt** [nelt]	**knelt** [nelt]	knien
to **know** [nəʊ]	**knew** [njuː]	**known** [nəʊn]	wissen, kennen
to **lead** [liːd]	**led** [led]	**led** [led]	führen
to **learn**	**learnt / learned**	**learnt / learned**	lernen
to **leave** [liːv]	**left** [left]	**left** [left]	verlassen
to **lend**	**lent**	**lent**	leihen
to **let**	**let**	**let**	lassen
to **lie**	**lay**	**lain**	liegen
to **light** [laɪt]	**lit** [lɪt] / **lighted** [ˈlaɪtɪd]	**lit** [lɪt] / **lighted** [ˈlaɪtɪd]	anzünden, anmachen
to **lose** [luːz]	**lost** [lɒst]	**lost** [lɒst]	verlieren
to **make**	**made**	**made**	machen, herstellen
to **mean** [miːn]	**meant** [ment]	**meant** [ment]	bedeuten
to **meet** [miːt]	**met** [met]	**met** [met]	(sich) treffen, kennenlernen
to **mow**	**mowed**	**mown / mowed**	mähen
to **pay**	**paid**	**paid**	bezahlen
to **put**	**put**	**put**	stellen
to **quit**	**quit**	**quit**	aufhören
to **read** [riːd]	**read** [red]	**read** [red]	lesen
to **rebuild**	**rebuilt**	**rebuilt**	wieder aufbauen
to **rewrite** [ˌriːˈraɪt]	**rewrote** [ˌriːˈrəʊt]	**rewritten** [ˌriːˈrɪtn]	umschreiben
to **ride** [raɪd]	**rode** [rəʊd]	**ridden** [ˈrɪdn]	fahren, reiten
to **ring**	**rang**	**rung**	klingeln, anrufen

infinitive	simple past	past participle	German
to **rise** [raɪz]	**rose** [rəʊz]	**risen** [ˈrɪzən]	ansteigen, (sich) erheben
to **run**	**ran**	**run**	laufen, rennen, leiten
to **say** [seɪ]	**said** [sed]	**said** [sed]	sagen
to **see**	**saw**	**seen**	sehen
to **sell**	**sold**	**sold**	verkaufen
to **send**	**sent**	**sent**	schicken
to **set**	**set**	**set**	setzen, stellen, legen
to **shake**	**shook**	**shaken**	schütteln
to **shine** [ʃaɪn]	**shone** [ʃɒn]	**shone** [ʃɒn]	scheinen
to **shoot** [ʃuːt]	**shot** [ʃɒt]	**shot** [ʃɒt]	schießen
to **show**	**showed**	**shown / showed**	zeigen
to **shrink**	**shrank**	**shrunk**	schrumpfen
to **sing**	**sang**	**sung**	singen
to **sink**	**sank**	**sunk**	sinken
to **sit**	**sat**	**sat**	sitzen
to **slay** [sleɪ]	**slew** [sluː]	**slain** [sleɪn]	töten; schlachten
to **sleep** [sliːp]	**slept** [slept]	**slept** [slept]	schlafen
to **smell**	**smelt / smelled**	**smelt / smelled**	riechen
to **speak** [spiːk]	**spoke** [spəʊk]	**spoken** [ˈspəʊkən]	sprechen
to **spend**	**spent**	**spent**	verbringen, ausgeben
to **split**	**split**	**split**	sich trennen
to **spoil**	**spoilt**	**spoilt**	verderben
to **spread**	**spread**	**spread**	sich ausbreiten, etw. verteilen

Appendix

IRREGULAR VERBS

infinitive	simple past	past participle	German
to **stand**	**stood**	**stood**	stehen
to **steal**	**stole**	**stolen**	stehlen
to **stick**	**stuck**	**stuck**	kleben
to **sting**	**stung**	**stung**	stechen
to **strike**	**struck**	**struck**	zuschlagen; treffen
to **strive** [straɪv]	**strove** [strəʊv]	**striven** [ˈstrɪvən]	sich bemühen
to **swim**	**swam**	**swum**	schwimmen
to **take**	**took**	**taken**	nehmen, dauern
to **teach** [tiːtʃ]	**taught** [tɔːt]	**taught** [tɔːt]	unterrichten
to **tear** [teə]	**tore** [tɔː]	**torn** [tɔːn]	reißen

infinitive	simple past	past participle	German
to **tell**	**told**	**told**	sagen, erzählen
to **think**	**thought**	**thought**	denken, glauben
to **throw**	**threw**	**thrown**	werfen
to **understand**	**understood**	**understood**	verstehen
to **wake up**	**woke up**	**woken up**	aufwachen
to **wear** [weə]	**wore** [wɔː]	**worn** [wɔːn]	tragen
to **weave**	**wove**	**woven**	weben
to **win** [wɪn]	**won** [wʌn]	**won** [wʌn]	gewinnen
to **withdraw**	**withdrew**	**withdrawn**	sich zurückziehen
to **write** [raɪt]	**wrote** [rəʊt]	**written** [ˈrɪtn]	schreiben

Acknowledgements

Audio credits

Dialogues produced by Anne Rosenfeld for RBA Productions, Brighton (rbaproductions.co.uk). Recording engineer Mark Smith.
Track 19: "Part-time woman". Text (OT): Shraya, Vivek. © Shraya, Vivek

Video credits

Video 1: produced by Anne Rosenfeld for RBA Productions, Brighton (rbaproductions.co.uk). Editor: David Rafique. Picture credits: akg-images / Erich Lessing; public domain sourced / access rights from IanDagnall Computing / Alamy Stock Photo; Pictorial Press Ltd / Alamy Stock Photo; Historical Images Archive / Alamy Stock Photo; GRANGER – Historical Picture Archive / Alamy Stock Photo; DB Pictures / Alamy Stock Photo

Picture credits

|Alamy Stock Photo, Abingdon/Oxfordshire: Aubert, Hans-Joachim 17.1; bilwissedition Ltd. & Co. KG 73.2; Casado, Marcos 70.1; Gess, Harold 46.1; Hero Images Inc. 22.1; Kipioro, Rut 56.1; Lebrecht Music & Arts 51.1; Negi, Umesh 23.1; PA Images 13.1; Pictorial Press Ltd 8.1; Science History Images 73.1; See Li/Picture Capital 67.1; Smith Archive 36.1; The Canadian Press 60.1; WENN Rights Ltd 64.1; World History Archive 34.1; Zoonar GmbH 26.1; ZUMA Press, Inc. 62.1. |Getty Images, München: AFP/Weiss, Angela 14.1; Bettmann 37.1; Eckenroth, Rodin 28.1; Gallo Images/Bopape, Oupa 47.1; Gallo Images/Sowetan 33.1; Hulton Archive/Hussein, Anwar 25.1; Squire, Jamie 38.1; Universal History Archive/UIG 7.1. |iStockphoto.com, Calgary: Dutta, Nisha 10.3; jacoblund 50.1; Sha, Shakeel 44.1. |Shutterstock.com, New York: Animaflora PicsStock 68.1; avijit bouri 18.1; Curioso.Photography 10.4; DestinaDesign 39.1; erichon 31.1; Feng Yu 74.1; Finn stock 48.1; freshcare 69.1; ingianima 72.1; JONATHAN PLEDGER 43.1; LBeddoe 80.1; Loniel 41.1; Mainka, Markus 57.1; Mariia, Domakhina 49.1; Moloko88 55.1; Morris, Ken 65.1; panoglobe 6.1; Prostock-studio 77.1; Rawpixel.com 81.1; ricochet64 15.1; Roxane 134 32.1; SeventyFour 19.1; Simoes, Arthur 10.2; sirtravelalot 71.1; Slatter, Andrea 45.1; Yuriy K 75.1. |Shutterstock.com (RM), New York: Moviestore 35.1. |stock.adobe.com, Dublin: Africa Studio 79.1; YellowCrest 10.1.

Text credits

p. 9 (abbreviated and adapted): Sheryl Sebastian, "Kamala Das – The Mother of Modern Indian English Poetry", Feminism in India, 31 March 2017, https://feminisminindia.com/2017/03/31/kamala-das-essay/ [29.08.2023]; **p. 21 (abbreviated and adapted):** Robert McCrum, "The 100 best novels: No 48 – A Passage to India by EM Forster (1924)", The Guardian, 18 August 2014, https://www.theguardian.com/books/2014/aug/18/100-best-novels-a-passage-to-india-em-forster-robert-mccrum [29.08.2023]; **pp. 28/29 (abbreviated):** Markus Fiedler, "What's love got to do with it? (2023) – Wie lustig ist eine arrangierte Heirat?", Kino-Zeit, https://www.kino-zeit.de/film-kritiken-trailer-streaming/whats-love-got-to-do-with-it-2023 [29.08.2023]; **p. 33 (abbreviated):** Sarah Bartlett, Winnie Madikizela-Mandela (1936 – 2018), Black Past, 4 October 2010, https://www.blackpast.org/global-african-history/mandela-winnie-madikizela-1936/ [29.08.2023]; **p. 38 (abbreviated and adapted):** Zeenat Mowzer, "10 SA female Paralympians who achieved glory despite the odds", news24, 18 September 2016, https://www.news24.com/life/archive/10-sa-female-paralympians-who-achieved-glory-despite-the-odds-20160918 [29.08.2023]; **p. 40:** Alan Paton, *Cry, the Beloved Country*, Penguin Books 1958, p. 11 (adapted), p. 20, p. 77; p. 51: *Coal Train*, Masekela, Hugh. Weve got rythm music/Kondor Musikverlag GmbH, Berlin; **pp. 52/53 (abbreviated):** Bartholomäus Grill, "Wie auf der Titanic, nur zappenduster: Wenn der Stromausfall zum Alltag gehört", Stern, 29.01.2013, https://www.stern.de/gesellschaft/erfahrungsbericht-suedafrika--unser-leben-ohne-strom-in-kapstadt-33142272.html [29.08.2023]; **p. 66 (abbreviated):** https://www.renolon.com/teenage-spending-statistics/, https://www.reference.com/world-view/much-money-average-teenager-spend-3fbb309f1fdb12af; **pp. 80/81 (abbreviated):** Robert Ferdinand Krieger, "Damit das Handy nicht zum Tatort wird", Rheinische Post, 22.08.2023, https://rp-online.de/nrw/staedte/mettmann/social-media-medienscouts-lotsen-durch-digitale-welt_aid-95924225 [14.09.2023]

Also see individual text credits in the audio script (webcodes).